Other books by Dr. Leanna E. Manuel

Don't Diet: Reprogram Your Weight with Meridian Tapping
©2012 ISBN 10: 1483931118 ISBN 13: 978-1483981116

Tap It Away: 10 Minutes to Freedom with EFT
©2011 ISBN 10: 1477558195 ISBN 13: 978-1477558195

UNLEASH YOUR PRIMAL POWER

Totem Tapping for Health and Happiness

Leanna Manuel, Psy.D.

BALBOA.
PRESS

A DIVISION OF HAY HOUSE

Balboa Press books may be ordered through booksellers or by contacting:

Balboa Press
A Division of Hay House
1663 Liberty Drive
Bloomington, IN 47403
www.balboapress.com
1 (877) 407-4847

Print information available on the last page.

ISBN: 978-1-9822-2606-0 (sc)
ISBN: 978-1-9822-2607-7 (e)

Balboa Press rev. date: 09/04/2019

This book is dedicated to the animals that have added so much meaning to my life. There have been so many, and I sadly don't remember the names of some of them. I do remember their essence and love. Thank you to Sandy, Traci, Ralph, Sigmund, Hank, Rita, Bob, Shadow, Kisu, and Bodhi.

Shadow 2002-2019

Contents

In the early 2000s, I found myself in over my head with my adopted daughter. She had accumulated a laundry list of diagnoses from a whole host of doctors who offered very few solutions to managing them. Desperate, anxious, and skeptical, I booked a family therapy appointment with Dr. Manuel and was pleasantly surprised to be greeted by her dog Shadow when we arrived. I tend to connect more quickly with dogs than with people, so knew I could focus my attention on Shadow instead of Dr. Manuel if she proved to be like those who had come before her. My daughter is not a big fan of animals, so she was less than thrilled, but Shadow calmly and quietly earned her trust and put her at ease. I wasn't a big fan of therapists at the time, but in much the same way Shadow had with my daughter, Dr. Manuel patiently earned my trust and put my mind at ease. We had finally found someone who meshed with us, who didn't look at my daughter as her diagnoses, who saw the people beneath the quirks, and who offered solutions to managing our day-to-day lives.

Our journey spanned years and many ups and downs. At the lowest point, I realized I needed individual therapy as much as my daughter did. By this time, Kisu had joined the pack at the office, and with Shadow sprawled across my feet and Kisu snuggled up against me, I felt comfortable enough to address some of my biggest fears as a mother and as a person. Just as the dogs didn't judge me, neither did Dr. Manuel, not even when I all but mocked her suggestion that I should try tapping for my anxiety. I had seen it work for my daughter but had chalked it up to the power of suggestion. I would not be as easily swayed by her hocus pocus. To debunk the tapping nonsense, I attended one of her evening workshops and found myself feeling ridiculous tapping on spots all over my upper body, which only made me more anxious. With her instruction, I kept tapping, and, lo and behold, my anxiety began to subside. But wouldn't it have naturally lessened on its own anyhow? I wasn't completely convinced either way, so I decided to try it later at home, on my own, with no outside influences. It worked. It still works. I don't always do it "right," but I have found there is no wrong way to tap once you understand the basics.

I used Dr. Manuel's first book, *Tap It Away*, published in 2012, to guide me through one of the most stressful times of my life. The year prior, I had traded my comfortable corporate job for waiting tables in order to devote my time to Project Believe, a budding nonprofit organization I founded to provide comfort and support to youth orphaned by mental, emotional, and behavioral challenges. It was Christmastime, and I needed to provide gifts for sixty-five foster children not living in foster homes and coordinate a one-hundred-person volunteer event while struggling to make ends meet and trying to carve out enough time for my own daughter. My anxiety was getting the best of me, and more than once, I wondered whether the reward was worth the risk I had taken the year before. I tapped my way through the book and the holidays and am proud to say it was worth every bit of blood, sweat, tears, and tapping. Over the next few years, we were able to support more than three hundred kids year-round, and we continue to grow!

It's been nearly a decade since the last time my daughter and I sat in Dr. Manuel's office as clients. At that time, Bob had joined forces with Shadow and Kisu by quite literally showing up at the office one day and never leaving. I felt a little like Bob, having just shown up years before and almost immediately knowing I had found "my pack." While distance separates us, I am honored to now call Lea my friend. She has supported Project Believe since its inception and is my trusted compass for remembering where and why we began. When I first learned about Lea's latest book idea to tie together tapping and animal totems, I was instantly filled with excitement and intrigue. I wanted to be the first to unleash my primal power! Unlike the skepticism I initially had for tapping, I have always felt a connection to animals and searched for their deeper meaning and symbolism in our lives.

My earliest totem animals were the owl and the deer. They have consistently shown up in my life, teaching me to channel the wisdom of the owl while trusting my intuition, like the deer.

It's the animals who have unexpectedly popped into my life that have delivered some of the most profound messages. While driving with a friend and her young son and four-month-old baby one night, we passed hundreds—maybe thousands—of frogs on the road. Knowing frogs symbolize fertility, rebirth, and transition, I jokingly told her she should take a pregnancy test to rule out fertility. She cursed me for even saying it aloud but took a test to pacify me the next day. She welcomed child number three later that year.

Unleash Your Primal Power: Totem Tapping for Health and Happiness will be a book I reference for a lifetime. Whether it's to build on the strength of my totem animals' characteristics, to better understand the unexpected animal-relayed messages that appear in my life, or to confront my own fears (that sometimes materialize as butterflies), I am grateful for this little gem. Pairing tapping with animal totems is a refreshing and brilliant new perspective. I hope you find just as much knowledge and happiness in it and because of it as I have.

Tammie Rafferty
Executive Director, Project Believe

1

Totem Tapping

Introduction

I have always loved animals and felt a strong connection to them. There are stories of me singing to a box turtle as a child to get it to come out of its shell. I've always had at least one dog and also used to have a dream of becoming a zookeeper. I spent hours watching the polar bears at the Columbus Zoo, and I was ecstatic when I went through the Penguin Encounter at the Newport Aquarium with my daughter-in-law and actually got to meet some of the penguins. On a trip to Washington, DC, I spent an entire day at the National Zoo watching the pandas.

On a different level, I've been attracted, as have so many other people, to animals in the media. I feel a kinship with the Winnie the Pooh characters and adore *The Jungle Book*, *The Lion King*, and other animated classics. I grew up with TV shows such as *Lassie*, *Flipper*, and *Rin Tin Tin*. In both my personal life and in my favorite media, animals have always been present.

Certain animals stand out as being lifelong objects of fascination, including polar bears, pandas, Canada geese, dogs, wolves, and hawks. I have also had strong aversions to spiders, most insects, opossums, and sharks. Other animals became important to me for shorter periods of time. I was once obsessed with frogs, and another time, it was turtles. For me, these were times of total immersion, and I now know that these animals had a message or something to teach me at that time in my life.

During my adult years, I met my dear friend Zach, who introduced me to the basics of Shamanism and totem animals. I was already aware of the Chinese Zodiac, some Egyptian mythology, and some Celtic symbology. This prepared me to more fully understand the connection between animal behavior, animal totems, and human existence. I have found comfort listening to the guidance of my totem animals and that of other animals that wander in and out of my life.

When I was writing *Tap It Away: 10 Minutes to Freedom with EFT*, I decided to utilize some of what I knew about totem animals to write a chapter called "Animal Wisdom." My purpose was to demonstrate how tapping doesn't have to be a stern and serious endeavor in order to get more work done. I also wanted to illustrate how challenges don't always need to be tackled head-on. It was perhaps the most enjoyable chapter that I wrote. I decided then that I would someday write another book that was entirely dedicated to tapping with totem animal characteristics. This book is a product of that long-ago decision.

Tapping and Totems Together

Mention any animal. I dare you to avoid conjuring an image, feeling, or characteristic associated with it. Animals are a powerful way to become aware of subconscious associations, personal motivations, and intrinsic desires because of the relative ease in eliciting these common representations. If I say that someone was a mouse, I'm sure you get an image of someone who is small or timid. If I refer to someone as being a real shark, you instantly have a reaction. More often than not, your reaction or association is going to be somewhat similar to mine, particularly if we are from similar cultures. These animal stereotypes exist for a reason.

The Native American Medicine Wheel was used, in part, as a method of self-knowledge and self-realization (Meadows, 2002). The word *medicine* in this context translates to energy or vital power. Therefore, a being's medicine was an expression of its energy system. We can use this energy to understand ourselves, discover our potential, find meaning or purpose in our lives, or simply take control of our destiny.

Obviously, there is not sufficient room within this book to include tapping examples for all of the animals, birds, and insects on this planet, and my purpose in writing this book is to stimulate you to unleash your own primal power. It would be impossible for me to guess what animals might be important to your growth and development. I considered using only animals that have been important in my own journey but eventually chose to include animals based on some more random factors, such as animals that happened to pop into my mind, literally ran across my path, were visited at the zoo, or were a favorite of someone I love.

Keep in mind that the primary goal of this text is to demonstrate how to use the animal totems for tapping, not necessarily to focus on the actual animals themselves. I believe there are enough examples to assist you in getting the hang of this.

If you already know what your animal totems or spirit animals might be, grab a piece of paper and write them down. If you don't already know what your totems or spirit animals are, write down your three or four favorite animals, your three or four least favorite animals, and perhaps an animal you have seen recently that isn't common in your usual daily life. Those all have a good chance of teaching you something important. I would encourage you to tap along with all of the examples, whether you think they might be your totems or not, because there may still be something to gain.

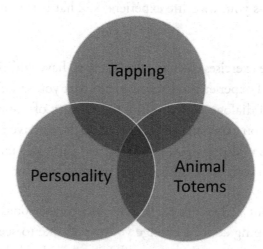

Figure 1 Venn Diagram illustrating overlap of Tapping, Personality, and Animal Totems. The techniques of Unleash Your Primal Power draw from that area of overlap.

How to Get the Most out of This Book

This book is intended for people with all levels of experience. Particularly at the beginning, there will be more frequent reminders about rating your emotional intensity before and after tapping as well as suggestions for getting more out of each tapping exercise. Those will gradually fade away once there have been quite a few examples to help you feel confident. If you are already an expert tapper, please excuse the procedural comments that are already familiar to you.

Some people will prefer to start at the beginning and work their way through the chapters, one after the other. This is probably the best option if you are new to tapping. There will be sufficient instructional material in the early chapters to get you started on your tapping journey. Other people may find it more enjoyable to skip around, choosing animals that interest them. In either case, please take the time to do the meditations and exercises associated with each chapter. While you may become more self-aware just from reading about the animal characteristics and the tapping examples, you are not likely to experience the lasting change that is possible when you tap.

The tapping meditations and scripts provided are examples to encourage you to chart your own path. The most effective tapping comes from your own thoughts and feelings. Some of the scripts that are provided will not appear to be relevant for you. In spite of this, I encourage you to tap along with each one. Then do it again, changing the words to better match your own experiences. Ultimately you will be able to recognize different ways to use these tapping examples to directly address your own life experiences. That is the real goal here—to get you tapping.

As you work through these exercises, you are also likely to have additional thoughts about the tapping phrases and related experiences. I recommend that you write them down. If you find yourself having an internal dialogue questioning the validity of a statement or exercise, write down your doubts. When you experience moments of clarity or have those *aha* moments, write them down too. Questions will pop up. Those are great things to tap on in the future, but if you don't write them down, you are less likely to remember to do it.

Then there are the "yes, buts." These are awesome fuel for personal change. They are likely to occur when you are tapping about a change you would like to see in your life. You get all excited and motivated; however, you find yourself saying "yes, but" about a challenge, obstacle, or nagging self-doubt that stands between you and your goal. You can keep tapping with your original plan or switch over to the "yes, but" right away. In either case, there will likely be something to jot down for later tapping practice. At this point, you are probably thinking that you could spend the entire day doing nothing but tapping. Just think how great you would feel after that!

Why Tapping?

The answer to this question can be summed up by this riddle. What has only two fingers and nine spots and can change your life forever? Of course, the answer is tapping.

The origin of tapping as I know it can be traced back to Thought Field Therapy (TFT), which was pioneered by Roger Callahan. Dr. Callahan was a classically trained psychologist and worked with patients presenting with a variety of issues. As the story goes, he had one patient with a very severe water phobia. I'm not talking about being afraid to go in the ocean; she couldn't take a shower. He tried all of the usual psychological techniques, and his patient continued to make very little progress. One day as he was working with her, she mentioned the feeling that she would get in the pit of her stomach whenever she saw any amount of water. Fortunately, Dr. Callahan had been studying some applied kinesiology principles and was aware of some of the acupuncture meridians. He asked his patient to tap under her eye, the acupuncture point associated with the stomach meridian in Chinese Medicine. After she had finished tapping she was able to approach a swimming pool full of water without fear and her water phobia didn't return. Dr. Callahan then expanded his work using acupuncture points to include other presenting problems and used additional spots for tapping.

Dr. Callahan's TFT technique was fairly complicated and required a specific sequence of tapping for different problems. That's where Gary Craig, founder of the Emotional Freedom Technique (EFT) comes in. He was a student of Dr. Callahan's, and after working with TFT for a while, condensed the system into something that was much more easily used. The basic system of EFT can be used for most, if not all, issues and generally yields tremendous results.

I was initially introduced to tapping while I was at an applied kinesiology conference in Florida. I was in a large conference area during break time and was waiting for the next speaker to get started. A man (I have no idea who it was) jumped up on a folding chair and told us about this great new technique he had just learned. He had the rest of us stand up on our chairs and notice how wobbly they were. Then he taught us to tap. We tapped until the feeling of being unsafe up on the chair went away. I got back down, listened to the next speaker, and went on with my life.

The experience did leave a lasting impression though, and I decided to do a little bit of investigation. That's when I found out about Gary Craig and The Emotional Freedom Technique (EFT). He was doing a seminar about this tapping thing in Flagstaff, Arizona, a few months later, so I signed up. My life, and hopefully now your life, was changed forever.

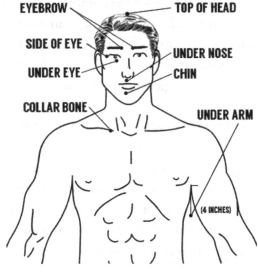

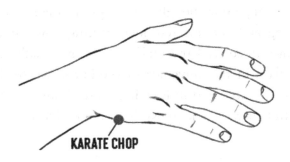

These tapping points are generally sufficient to address most people's issues. When you tap on these spots, you will tap gently on the area with your fingertips for approximately seven taps.

Meridian tapping can be broken into six easy steps (which will be described in much more detail later):

1. Make a statement that describes what needs to change. Many people call this the Most Pressing Issue," or MPI. I also sometimes call it the "problem statement" or "starting statement."
2. Rate the emotional intensity associated with that change statement.

3. Repeat a Setup Phrase while tapping the karate-chop point.
4. Tap on the meridians using the tapping points and a Reminder Phrase.
5. Repeat the original problem statement or MPI.
6. Rate the intensity again.

Let's practice finding the tapping spots just to see how it feels. Tap five to nine times on each of the tapping points. Refer back to the chart if you need to. Nothing bad will happen if you tap fewer than five or more than nine times. You also don't have to tap hard, but tap firmly enough to feel it. It shouldn't cause any pain or discomfort.

When I first started tapping, I had the thought that if a little bit was good, a lot more would be better. I tapped more often, and I tapped harder. I didn't notice any problem, and I was getting great results. Then I went to see my massage therapist, and she noticed that I had little bruises under my arms. They were very small, round bruises, and at first, I didn't know how I could have gotten them. I didn't remember any injury. Later, it dawned on me. These bruises were from my own fingertips when I was doing the tapping. I reduced the pressure and saved myself from further injury, and the tapping still worked just as well.

Setup Phrases

Setup Phrases can be a very useful prelude to meridian tapping and include a statement of the problem as well as a positive affirmation. There are many ways to construct a Setup Phrase. It can be a simple statement of the most pressing issue, such as "I am hungry," or something much more complex, such as a rambling exploration of a problem that is not yet clearly defined in your mind. You will find examples of both types of Setup Phrases in the tapping exercises throughout the book. The affirmation is what helps to prepare the body's energy system for change. A traditional affirmation used in this kind of work is "I deeply and completely love and accept myself." Even though it is simple, it really works well. Other people find that expanding the affirmation feels more useful. This might include a choice statement that outlines what the desired resolution to the problem might be.

To be honest, I don't always use a Setup Phrase. If the emotion that I am tapping about is happening to me in the current moment, I often just start tapping on the points. I find this to be very effective.

Reminder Phrases

Reminder Phrases are usually shortened versions of the problem statement that can serve to keep us focused. People have very strong defense mechanisms that are generally useful to help us avoid the pain of our own circumstances. Although we say we want to resolve our problems, our natural tendency is to avoid or distract ourselves from the discomfort. Reminder Phrases help us to prevent our minds from wandering away from the issue. If you use our previous problem statement of "I am hungry," an example of a Reminder Phrase could be "this hunger" and would help to keep you focused.

With both the Setup Phrases and the Reminder Phrases, people often get very hung up on the words. I frequently get asked, "How important are the words?" That is actually a pretty complex question, and the answer depends upon the situation. As I said with Setup Phrases, if what I'm tapping about is happening right now, I don't think the words are terribly important, and I often don't say anything; I just tap. All you need is some emotional honesty. If I am working on any issue, emotion, or situation that isn't happening right at that moment, I do use the words. Please remember—you can't do it wrong! Any words you use are perfect. If you see videos or live demonstrations of tapping, you may see the coach using pretty interesting language, neurolinguistic techniques, and combination techniques that have been gleaned from their professional experience. Those things are nice but not necessary. Let me reassure you that tapping without them can still be quite effective.

Basic Negative Sequence

When I first learned meridian tapping, it was in the form of The Emotional Freedom Technique (EFT) as taught by Gary Craig. The Setup Statements and tapping sequences followed a basic format that is highly effective. The EFT Setup Phrase, which is a basic statement of the problem, is repeated three times while you tap on the karate-chop point. This is followed by "I deeply and completely love and accept myself." The Reminder Phrases are shortened versions of the problem statement and are repeated at each of the tapping points. This repetitive sequence of Setup Phrase and Reminder Phrases is continued until the intensity rating is significantly reduced or eliminated. Any thought or feeling that comes into your awareness can be plugged into this simple formula:

Even though (insert thought or feeling here), I deeply

and completely love and accept myself.

Then you can say the thought or feeling as you tap on each of the other tapping points. If it is a long thought or feeling, you can shorten it to just a few key words that will keep you focused on the problem at hand.

Gary is a true master of his craft with amazing skill and expertise, but the technique really couldn't be any easier. If you follow this format, you are likely to have amazing results even without his remarkable intuition and years of experience.

These Setup Statements and Reminder Phrases are negative statements. They are not intended to be positive. The negative statements and phrases act as the keys to unlock the negative energy that is trapped in our energy system and can play an important part in reclaiming our emotional freedom, resolving problems, and enhancing our well-being.

People are sometimes uncomfortable with these negative statements, particularly if they are familiar with the practice of affirmations or are aware of the Law of Attraction. They ask, "Aren't the negative statements attracting more negativity?" No! If you stay in the negative state, I would agree, but in tapping, we are using this negative statement as an honest report of what we are feeling. That is the energy that you are already putting out in the universe, even if you might be saying what you consider to be the right thing.

This is the time to be absolutely honest with yourself. Try to think of it this way: you can't get to Point B if you aren't honest with yourself about where Point A, your starting point, is. The negative statement is Point A. We don't intend to stay there. We just need to be honest about our current feeling or situation so that we can chart a course for change.

Positive Tapping

Although EFT purists say that it isn't necessary, many variations of tapping that include additional positive affirmations are popular and tremendously successful. I have found that the best time to add some positive affirmations while tapping is after you have tapped on the negative statements for a while and your intensity has lowered considerably. I personally do not recommend positive tapping until your negative intensity rating is at a three or lower, although you will see it included earlier in many of the examples that follow just for illustration. There will be much more later about these ratings, so don't get hung up on it just now.

Look back at the earlier problem statement (MPI) of "I am hungry." We could substitute "I choose to follow my eating plan with confidence" instead of "I deeply and completely love and accept myself." This type of choice statement, made popular by Dr. Patricia Carrington (Carrington, 2001), is very empowering. It extends to the Reminder Phrases as well. Some of the negative Reminder Phrases can be replaced with the new resolution or choice statement, but again, I don't recommend rushing this. Stick with the negative until almost all of the truth of that negative statement is gone.

To continue the previous example, the positive tapping can be our Point B. This is where we want to go. We can use the final destination if it doesn't seem too outlandish or we can use some closer checkpoints along the way, just like you would on any long trip.

We can also use positive tapping when we are confused about something. If I used the Reminder Phrase of "looking for clarity," I wouldn't consider that a negative statement. I often use tapping this way when I read something that I don't understand or when I am not sure what my own personal view on a subject might be. Try it. It is a great tool.

Intensity Ratings

I first became aware of rating scales when I was working as a nurse. It was quite common to ask someone to rate their pain. Sometimes, we used a five-point scale and sometimes a ten-point scale, but the purpose was always the same. We were trying to get a way to measure someone's experience at a distinct point in time. Not only was that useful in determining what intervention to use, but it was also valuable in judging the effectiveness of the treatment. During my clinical psychology training, we frequently constructed and used rating scales. Psychology rating scales are commonly used for rating emotions and work the same way as the pain scales.

The process of rating the intensity of the feeling when engaged in meridian tapping is not essential but can be very useful. It can give you a snapshot of your current experience. It becomes particularly beneficial when the feeling changes. Instead of noticing our relief, many people move very quickly on to the next problem or an aspect of the original problem that wasn't being worked on. Then instead of noticing how well meridian tapping worked and how much better we feel, we mistakenly believe that nothing has happened and might even give up on using the technique.

Sometimes, when our intensity about a topic drops dramatically, we feel so much better that we do not finish the process. It is a tremendous relief to go from an intensity level of ten, where you can feel the distress in your whole body down to a level of five or six. If you stop there, you will continue to feel better but not as good as if you had continued tapping and made the issue go away completely. The ratings can help you stay in touch with what you are really feeling and can be a useful guide for knowing when to continue or when to stop.

The rating scale that I commonly use is identified by the acronym SUDs. It stands for Subjective Units of Distress scale (Wolpe, 1969). This scale is defined by the user so there is lot of variation. When I label my feeling as a ten, it will not be exactly the same as what you might rate as a ten. If you are asked to rate the intensity of a bad feeling, with ten being the worst, it is generally useful to give your first impression and not overthink it. It can also be helpful to flip the scale around, particularly when you are tapping about something that you want to increase. I find it helpful to think of ten being the most of something (either good or bad) and zero being the least of something (either good or bad). For highly visual people, seeing the scale as a thermometer can be effective. The low intensity would probably be visualized as a low temperature and high intensity would be visualized as a high temperature.

Another useful scale is the Validity of Cognition scale (VoC). This was developed by Francine Shapiro, PhD, and is a measure of our confidence in a belief. It is a seven-point scale in which seven represents the feeling that something is totally believable, and one is totally unbelievable. I still use this as a ten-point scale just to keep things simple.

Unfortunately, many people get hung up on the rating, much like they do with the words. They may have difficulty assigning a value, or worry about what will happen if they use the wrong number. There is no such thing as the wrong number. As previously mentioned, the amount of feeling, intensity, or distress that you experience is subjective. It is relevant only to you and depends on many factors, including your previous experiences, your tolerance to pain and discomfort, and the context of your current experience.

Before I had experienced knee surgery, I might have assigned an intensity level of ten to a physical pain, believing that it was the worst pain anyone could ever experience. My experience of the pain was real. Then came knee surgery. Looking back, the previous physical pain would have only been a six. Knee surgery pain became my new gold standard for measuring physical pain intensity. I hope that I never experience anything that makes me re-evaluate whether knee surgery was a ten or not, but who knows? The same is true for emotional states. It can be difficult to rate sadness. People who experience the grief of losing a beloved pet really are sad. They may experience it as a nine or ten at the time but can acknowledge that in comparison to the sadness of losing a child or spouse, it might be lower, but they don't have a personal frame of reference.

The exact number doesn't matter. It isn't going to be judged by anyone. It is your own personal experience, which cannot be wrong. Don't let the intensity rating derail you. I have a tapping exercise for you that may help with any confusion or difficulty you may be having about this. If you are still uncomfortable with ratings after you have tapped a few times—skip them when tapping along in this book. After you have more experience with tapping, you can go back and try the ratings again. It is much more important to do the tapping than to worry about the ratings.

Exercise

Before tapping through this exercise, please review the tapping charts and then say this problem statement aloud: "I can't rate the intensity." Is this a little true or a lot true for you? Repeat this Setup Statement three times while tapping on the karate-chop point on the side of your hand. "Even though I can't seem to rate the intensity of my feeling or experience, I deeply and completely love and accept myself." Now tap along using each of the eight tapping points.

Tapping Point	Reminder Phrase
Eyebrow	Can't rate the intensity
Side of the eye	Problem with ratings
Under the eye	Not sure about the intensity
Under the nose	Nervous about assigning a number
Chin	It might not be right
Collarbone	Afraid to rate the intensity
Under the arm	Can't rate the intensity
Top of the head	Problem with the ratings

Take a deep breath, and let it out slowly. Do you feel better? If not, do it again or move on to the next section.

Psychological Reversal

When I first started learning about meridian tapping, there was a great emphasis placed on psychological reversal. People had lots of different metaphors to explain it. I tend to think of psychological reversal (PR) as a mental program that causes the opposite reaction from what is expected. Have you ever had the experience of saying that you want to lose weight and then almost immediately you eat a large bowl of ice cream or a candy bar? That is not what you would expect to happen if you say you want to lose weight. It is like there is some internal program running behind the scenes that has control over your behavior and your destiny.

Many people describe this as a spiritual or energetic issue, but no matter how you describe it, the result is the same. People who are experiencing PR don't have the results they want and often sabotage their own success. Galo and Vincenzi (2000) describe six different types of self-sabotage or PR. These include massive reversal, deep-level reversal, specific reversal, criteria-related reversal, mini-reversal, and recurring reversal. Massive reversals impact most, if not all, of the major areas of life functioning. Economics, relationships, mood, jobs—they all seem to be chronically going wrong. People experiencing deep-level reversal typically believe that the problem or situation they want to change is bigger or more powerful than they are able to manage. Individuals experiencing specific reversal don't have problems in so many different areas of their lives. Instead, they have something going on in just one area, such as a specific phobia.

Criteria-related reversals are another type of reversal in which the problem seems to be specific rather than existing in many life domains. This type commonly involves some sort of thought process or programming, such as shame or guilt, that prevents making a change. The person may feel unworthy of their desired goal. The fifth type of reversal that Gallo and Vincenzi describe is the mini-reversal. You can think of this as a form of back-sliding. This occurs when you are making progress toward your goal and then stop moving forward or even take a few steps back. I struggle frequently with this type. Finally, they describe the recurring reversal. Unlike the mini-reversal, this is a return of the problem, going all the way back to the starting point. If you are like me, you have experienced at least two or three of these different types in your life.

The types appear to differ in the ways that they have developed and in the scope of their impact. What these different types have in common is their interference with optimal functioning.

Another thing that these different types of PR have in common is that they can be reduced or eliminated using meridian tapping.

The basic tapping procedure that you have already learned usually begins with tapping on the karate-chop point on the side of your hand and saying a statement about the problem followed by an affirmation about yourself. This is designed to help with PR. You may not have experienced it yet, but people with PR often have a moment of reticence or discomfort when they are confronted with the statement, "I deeply and completely love and accept myself" or any other variation of that phrase.

Imagine that you have a deep-level reversal in which you believe that overcoming your food addiction is something that is out of your grasp because it is too big or has too much of a hold on you, and you cannot imagine your life with food being any different than it is now. That's going on deep inside, perhaps even at the subconscious level. Then one day, you look in the mirror and say, "I'm unhappy with the way I look so I'm going to start my diet tomorrow." Does that sound familiar? In that moment, you really mean it. You just aren't aware that there is a deep-level reversal program running in the background that is keeping you stuck. Next, a well-meaning friend who has heard about this tapping thing suggests you try it. You think, *Why not? I've tried everything else.* Your friend teaches you about the tapping points, and you enthusiastically start tapping on your karate-chop point saying, "Even though I have this food addiction, I deeply and completely love and accept myself." Those last words are likely to barely come out in a whisper, if they come out at all. I have seen people sneeze, choke, cough, or freeze up completely when confronted with saying those words out loud. That is a clue that there is PR at work.

Mini-reversals are also very common when working with lifestyle issues. I certainly have experienced many weeks and months of clean, healthy eating only to suddenly find myself standing in the pantry stuffing potato chips into my mouth. When I came to my senses, I was not only mortified to look at how many calories I had just consumed but also how quickly the reversal came upon me. At first, I was completely blindsided and had no idea what the issue was. This change seemed to come out of the blue. After several rounds of tapping, I was not only able to identify the issue, but I was also able to see solutions.

Moving past PR isn't always easy. Particularly for people with massive reversal, deep-level reversal, and recurring reversal, professional help can be useful or necessary to move forward. We don't get this way overnight, and we usually have an abundance of help in developing our maladaptive thoughts and behaviors so it makes sense that we might need help to get rid of them as well. Particularly when working with PR, please remember to seek professional assistance if your symptoms seem to be getting worse or if the energy work becomes overwhelming to you.

Gamut Procedure

Have you ever heard the expression *run the gamut*? I have heard it and used it but only understood it through context, never knowing a dictionary definition. *Merriam-Webster* defines it as "to encompass an entire range of something." Synonyms include *range*, *spectrum*, *span*, *scope*, *breadth*, *scale*, or *extent*. *Gamut* is also a term that can apply in meridian tapping. While it is the name of a tapping spot, to me, it also relates to increasing the breadth and scope of your tapping, or "getting the whole thing."

There is a spot on the back of the hand between the knuckles at the base of the ring finger and little finger. It is the third point on the Triple Warmer acupuncture meridian, which is responsible for turning on and off the fight-flight-freeze response. It is also associated with the spleen meridian. Carol Prentice, in her article at www.thetappingsolution, describes the use of the Nine-Gamut Procedure. She indicates that disturbances in spleen energy may be involved in both physical and emotional problems.

The 9-Gamut Procedure was taught as an important component of the Emotional Freedom Technique decades ago when I was first learning it. For some reason I don't completely understand, many practitioners stopped teaching it regularly. Actually, so did I. It was the part of the tapping procedure that looked the strangest, and I feared that it prevented people from actually wanting to do the technique. Recently, I have revisited that decision and have decided to include it again in my own tapping. Other Energy Psychologists, such as Fred Gallo and Harry Vincenzi, in their book *Energy Tapping*, use a form of this procedure and call it "Brain Balancer." This is a very accurate label for what the 9-Gamut Procedure does.

The 9-Gamut Procedure includes these steps:

Tap the Gamut spot on the back of the hand continuously

1. Close your eyes tightly.
2. Open your eyes wide.

3. Without moving your head, look hard down to the right, as if trying to see your right hip.
4. Without moving your head, look hard down to the left, as if trying to see your left hip.
5. Without moving your head, circle your eyes clockwise.
6. Without moving your head, circle your eyes counter-clockwise.
7. Hum a few seconds of a tune, such as "Happy Birthday" or "Row Your Boat."
8. Count to five slowly.
9. Hum a few seconds of a tune, such as "Happy Birthday," or "Row Your Boat."

At this point, most people seem to want some explanation of why they are being encouraged to do this. Eye movements are tied to brain function. So, when you look right, you are using the left side of your brain, and when you look left, you are using the right side of your brain. Similarly, humming stimulates the right side of the brain, and counting stimulates the left side of the brain. When you put this all together, you stimulate the whole brain, while also changing the emotional response by tapping on the gamut spot.

Mair Llewellyn posted an interesting article on www.emofree.com that describes the pros and cons of using the Nine-Gamut Procedure. The cons are pretty much what I had expected: it takes longer, looks weird, and can be intimidating to new tappers. One advantage is that it is a method for tying tapping to other healing practices that people may have heard of, such as neurolinguistic programming (NLP), EMDR, and other brain-balancing techniques that are increasingly popular in the media. Another advantage is that the blocks to change/healing seem to break down more quickly when it is used and previously unconscious memories can be unlocked. The third advantage that she identifies is the silent period during the Nine-Gamut, which provides a break from the words often used while tapping the other points. In this silence, self-awareness and insight have a chance to bloom. Lastly, the gamut point itself is quite useful whenever there is pain or emotional trauma. As I stated before, it is associated with that fight-flight-freeze response that is a part of the trauma/pain experience.

Still not convinced? Dawson Church, an amazing practitioner and researcher, published an article on *EFT Universe* that shared research from University of South Florida that looked at eye movements in a sample of people with PTSD and depression. Researchers found that the emotional distress held in memories of traumatic events was rapidly reduced while using Accelerated Resolution Therapy (ART). ART also uses eye movements similar to the Nine-Gamut Procedure. While the exact mechanism for change is still under study, research indicates that many different techniques that use eye movements have been clinically useful in reducing emotional distress.

Ready to give it a try?

1. Do a setup statement while tapping on the karate-chop point as usual.
2. Do a round of tapping using your reminder statement.
3. Before doing your second round of tapping, locate your gamut spot (either hand) between the knuckles of your ring finger and little finger and about a half-inch onto the back of your hand, and start tapping.
4. Do the eye movements, humming, and counting.
5. Then continue your tapping as usual.
6. Repeat as desired

Animal Totems

> The idea that we know ourselves through animals appears again and again in the theories of the origins of consciousness. Some people say the animals once had all the knowledge and transmitted it to us … Others say that human self-awareness begins in the caves, when our grandfathers and grandmothers marked the walls with animal images, making the first move from only-literal to also-imaginal.
>
> —James Hillman

It is my understanding that in Native American tradition, as well as other cultures, a totem can be a spirit being, sacred object, or symbol. Think of it as any object or being that you feel closely associated with and that has some relationship to your life. A totem animal is one that is with you as a guide throughout your life, both in the physical and spiritual realms. This totem offers power and wisdom to the individual who is open to learning. Some people just know what their totem animals are. There are also other animals or totems that can show up in our lives in a specific place or at a specific time that can help us learn and grow.

For those who are not ready to jump into the spiritual realm of totems, you can think of these animals as metaphors, fables, or symbols that are available to teach us an important lesson. There is also the view that animals are messengers sent directly from the spiritual world. Your choice in frame of reference can be based on your own belief system, and there is much to be gained with either approach. I personally believe that our Creator uses everything available in the Universe to communicate with us, and that includes the animals.

In the book *Spirit Animals*, Hal Zina Bennett describes the Zuni belief about how animal and human forms manifest in different ways. Bennet writes, "*Wolfness* is manifest in the animal we call wolf. But it is also manifest in human actions, in the shapes of certain rocks, and in numerous other ways. That is the essence of what we are acknowledging as we use the *animalness* to aid in our own development.*"

Ted Andrews, in the book *Animal-Wise: The Spirit Language and Signs of Nature*, opens chapter 1 by saying that everyone has a story of animals. What seems to be variable is whether these stories are positive or negative. Further, it is our reliance on reasoning or cognition that has interfered with our ability to live in harmony with the rest of nature. This is in contrast to the belief of the twelfth-century monk, Saint Francis of Assisi, that God's spirit lives in all of nature. If we accept that premise as true, it stands to reason that we can learn about ourselves, God, or others from all of creation. He also writes that animals aid in our spiritual development, and guide us in breaking down old barriers and accepting what is new.

Totems are found in many different cultures. For example, in China, the rabbit has been associated with mood and good luck and the snake has been associated with rebirth and renewal. There is a tale from the Kalahari Bushmen of Africa about how praying mantis wisdom guided them to pay attention to their dreams and reminded them that big things can come from small sources.

Some of the more common Egyptian totems include jackals, cats, scarab beetles, and crocodiles. The jackal was a symbol of the god Anubis who had the head of a jackal and was able to tell a good heart from a bad heart. This perhaps was because the jackal was able to tell good meat from bad when eating a carcass. Cats were also important animals in ancient Egypt. They were a symbol for Bast, the goddess of protection and warrior daughter and defender of Ra. She was also the goddess of the sunrise, music, dance, pleasure, family, fertility, and birth.

Scarab beetles, or kheper, were associated with the Egyptian god Khepri. It was said that Khepri pushed the sun across the sky, just as the kheper pushed balls of dung across the earth. The scarab beetle became a symbol of rebirth, including rebirth after death. For that reason, when Egyptians mummified a body, they would put a stone carved like the beetle in the place of the mummy's heart.

Crocodiles were both respected and feared. This makes sense given that the Nile was full of them. They were represented by the god Sobek, who possessed the strength and nature of the crocodile.

The Celts believed that there was energy and magic associated with nature. They felt that animals could remind us of desirable qualities, and they attempted to draw upon this power in their lives. The bull was revered among Celtic animals and symbolized strong will and stubbornness. It was also a sign of virility for men and fertility for women. The butterfly in Celtic tradition represents transformation, as it does it many cultures. Butterflies were used as a symbol with which to decorate birthing gowns, blankets, and bedsheets to help with a smooth transition when babies were being born.

The cat represented the guardian of the Underworld. They were thought to be stoic, silent, mysterious, crafty, and clever and able to grant insight into esoteric and ethereal knowledge. The dog symbolized loyalty and a strong bond of companionship between humans and animals. Having a dog in the village was considered good luck and a talisman of good health. The Celts also honored the magic of the dolphin. Dolphins became a symbol of friendship, intelligence, and good luck, perhaps because they were usually spotted when the weather was good and the seas were calm.

As with animal totems from any culture, it can be tempting to consider a certain animal symbol as good or bad, but I encourage you to refrain from quick judgment. Think about a time when you went to a Chinese restaurant with friends, and while waiting, you looked at the placemat to check out the zodiac symbols. Before finding which animal your birth year was associated with, you may have wished, much like Harry Potter—not Slytherin. This is likely due to the strong association of snakes with danger, Satan, or deception. It is important to remember that the snake is also associated with rebirth, renewal, intelligence, and problem-solving. I recently experienced a strong reaction when I plugged in my birth year for an online calculator, and it said my Chinese sign was pig. I felt amazingly let down because I believed I was born in the year of the dog, an animal that I have a strong affinity for. Fortunately, when I did it a second time, it said year of the dog. In spite of my knowledge that both the pig and the dog have positive and negative characteristics if not in balance, I fell prey to the same discrimination that I'm urging against.

So, are you ready? It is time to just jump in and *do it*! Don't be shy! Let's go!

2 Chapter

Ant

Did you know that there are more than ten thousand ant species? I didn't. I knew that there were red ones, brown ones, black ones, ants that bite, and ants that don't. Ants are social insects and usually live in communities that have a queen ant. The worker ants are female. They have no wings and don't reproduce, but have many duties within the colony, such as foraging for food, caring for the queen's baby ants, and protecting the community. Male ants have only one job—making baby ants with the queen. After they are done with that task, they usually die.

Not very long ago, I had an interesting infestation of ants in my kitchen. Actually, it really wasn't an infestation with swarms of ants everywhere; it was more of a constant trickle. I did some cleaning, and they seemed to be gone. That lasted about three hours, and then I saw another one walking across the kitchen floor. A few hours later, I saw one walking across a kitchen counter.

I don't harbor an intense dislike of ants, and I don't usually go out of my way to kill them if they are outside, but I don't want them on my kitchen counters or in my drawers, and I don't want to squish them under my bare feet when walking in the kitchen. Since they broke our "agreement" to stay outside, I decided to spray the baseboards to try to stop them from coming in. That lasted for about eight hours, then more ants.

While this ant battle was going on, I was also having some struggles at work. I felt that I was being treated as insignificant, not being allowed to exercise my own judgment and creativity, and just felt that I was generally not appreciated. On the inside, I was rebelling about all of this and was trying to assert my individualism within a culture that clearly doesn't value that.

The ants kept coming, and I continued to feel dissatisfied. One morning, while doing my lap swim, I had the thought, *What if the ants are acting as one of my totems?* I started thinking about the ant characteristics that I'd been writing about and became even more certain of it. I phoned a friend and shared my insight, thinking that it was hilarious that I had overlooked this possibility. I quipped, "Wouldn't it be hysterical if the ants were gone when I get home?" After all, I had finally received the message about being industrious, fitting in, stamina, and perseverance.

When I got home, the ants were indeed gone. I'm sure that I have more work to do pertaining to managing employment while nurturing my own dreams. I am glad the ants were persistent and that I finally caught on. It does make me wonder how many other times there have been animal totems willing to point me in the right direction, but I somehow missed out on getting the message.

To get started, let's do a tapping meditation to get in touch with some of the characteristics associated with ants and to get ready for whatever messages ants might have for you.

Tapping Meditation

Eyebrow	Ant
Side of the eye	Social
Under the eye	Ant
Under the nose	Colony
Chin	Ant
Collarbone	Solves complex problems
Under the arm	Ant
Top of the head	Interactive
Eyebrow	Ant
Side of the eye	Industrious
Under the eye	Ant

Under the nose	Cooperative effort
Chin	Ant
Collarbone	Hard work
Under the arm	Ant
Top of the head	Group-minded
Eyebrow	Ant
Side of the eye	Perseverance
Under the eye	Ant
Under the nose	Self-discipline
Chin	Ant
Collarbone	Teamwork
Under the arm	Ant
Top of the head	Orderly
Eyebrow	Ant
Side of the eye	Stamina
Under the eye	Ant
Under the nose	Honor
Chin	Ant
Collarbone	What message do you have for me?
Under the arm	Ant
Top of the head	Open to the message of ants

Keep tapping while considering the knowledge, experiences, and meaning that the ant may have for you. Be sure to write down any thoughts, beliefs, or feelings that arise when you have finished the tapping meditation. Which characteristics of the ant would you want more of? Which characteristics do you have in abundance?

For me, the ant is a fairly neutral symbol. I was raised on the image of ants being a nuisance when they visit a picnic. I have also seen the painful bites or stings from fire ants. I've been intrigued by anthills and loved the movie *Ants*. I even had an ant farm when I was growing up.

Ants are actually pretty important in Native American culture and lore. The Hopi, Pueblo, and Akimal O'odham tribes have Ant Clans. The Cherokee celebrate with an Ant Dance. In the Cahuilla creation myth, ants spread the earth out for people and animals to live upon. In a Hopi myth, the ant people provided shelter to the humans during the destruction of the First World. The industriousness and cooperative spirit associated with ants is often the focus of these stories.

Ants are also a common feature in literature. Ants are mentioned in the Bible and in the Quran. Ants were featured in *A Tramp Abroad* by Mark Twain, *The Once and Future King* by T. H. White, *Les Fourmis* by Bernard Werber, and *The Empire of the Ants* by H. G. Wells. Do you remember the cartoon *Atom Ant*? Did you have an ant farm when you were growing up? Did you play the game Ants in the Pants? Maybe you are more familiar with the movie *Antz* by Dream Works Animation in which Z-4195 longs for the opportunity to express himself or the movie *A Bug's Life* from Pixar Animation Studios in which the misfit ant Flik fancies himself to be an individualist and inventor.

The tapping exercises that follow draw from some of the common traits that are associated with real ants and with ants as a totem symbol.

I'm a Follower

Ant energy is associated with being part of a group and working for the good of the whole colony. Every ant knows that they are working for the queen ant and the entire group. Say this statement aloud: "I'm a follower." How true does that feel to you on the 0–10 SUD scale? Ten would be really true, and zero would be not true at all.

Setup (karate-chop point)—Even though I would rather be one of the workers instead of being in charge, even of my own destiny, I deeply and completely love and accept myself. Even though I would rather wait for directions than decide what to do for myself, I deeply and completely love and accept all of my feelings, thoughts, and behaviors. Even though I would rather be an ant, climbing endlessly in and out of the anthill and following directions, I deeply and completely love and accept myself.

Eyebrow	I am like an ant
Side of the eye	I take orders
Under the eye	I get the work done
Under the nose	I never get tired of taking orders
Chin	I'm very content to let others tell me what to do
Collarbone	I could never decide for myself

Under the arm	This way, I never have to be responsible
Top of the head	That feels safe to me
Eyebrow	There is safety in numbers
Side of the eye	The person in charge is the one taking the risk
Under the eye	Not me
Under the nose	I never have any good ideas anyway
Chin	I never figure things out on my own
Collarbone	That's not really true
Under the arm	I could probably decide a few things for myself
Top of the head	I could probably take responsibility more often
Eyebrow	I might not have to go in and out of the anthill all of the time
Side of the eye	I could sometimes be at the front of the line
Under the eye	I can switch back and forth between following and leading
Under the nose	Even if I don't want to be responsible for others
Chin	I could be responsible for myself
Collarbone	I don't really need someone to blame
Under the arm	I can take responsibility for myself
Top of the head	That feels safe to me

Take a deep breath, and let it out. Say the problem statement (MPI) aloud again—"I'm a follower"—and rerate the truthfulness. Notice any change.

What does it mean to you to be a follower? Perhaps that is something you are comfortable with but maybe not. Feel free to keep tapping with the previous script or add your own thoughts and feelings as you become aware of them.

Monotony

It appears that the life of an ant is repetitive. Are there times when monotony has been an issue in your life? Say this statement aloud: "I'm tired of the monotony of my life." How true does that statement feel to you on the 0 to 10 SUD scale? Write down your response.

Setup (karate-chop point)—I'm tired of the same-old, same-old. Every day is just like the one before and will probably be the same as tomorrow too. Even though I am tired of the monotony,

I love myself. Even though I hate doing the same thing over and over again day after day, I accept myself and acknowledge these feelings. Even though I'm tired of the repetitive pattern, I'm okay.

Eyebrow	This monotony
Side of the eye	Makes me tired
Under the eye	Same old thing
Under the nose	Over and over again
Chin	This monotony
Collarbone	Life is so repetitive
Under the arm	Today is just like yesterday
Top of the head	Tomorrow will be just like today
Eyebrow	This monotony
Side of the eye	I think I might be ready for a change
Under the eye	But probably not
Under the nose	I think I might be ready to see something different
Chin	But probably not
Collarbone	I would like to be open to new possibilities
Under the arm	But probably not
Top of the head	This monotony

Take a deep breath, and let it out. Say the starting statement aloud, "I'm tired of the monotony of my life." Rate it again on the SUD scale. Did you notice any change? What thoughts or feelings surfaced? It may be useful to continue tapping if your SUD rating remained high.

I'm Expendable

Even though some people may try to downplay their importance, I think most of us want to think that we are important to someone or something. I certainly do. While each ant carries out tasks that are important to the colony, the truth is that most are expendable.

Say this statement aloud: "I'm expendable." How true does that feel to you on the 0–10 SUD scale? In this case, ten would be really true and zero would be not true at all.

Setup (karate-chop point)—I'm feeling expendable, easily replaced, and almost disposable at work. That's a pretty uncomfortable feeling for me. Even though I am feeling this way, I choose to believe that I can work through this. Even though I don't like feeling expendable and disposable, I deeply and completely accept myself. Even though I feel pretty easily replaced at work, I am open to more clarity.

Eyebrow	Feeling expendable
Side of the eye	Feeling disposable
Under the eye	Expendable and disposable
Under the nose	Not very comfortable
Chin	Not what I'm used to
Collarbone	I was actually called a commodity
Under the arm	It felt demeaning
Top of the head	I'm doing a good job in my position
Eyebrow	And I get positive feedback on my work
Side of the eye	But something is missing
Under the eye	Very few people have tried to get to know me
Under the nose	There's a difference between being appreciated for being me
Chin	Versus being thankful someone, anyone, is doing the job
Collarbone	I really want it to be more about me
Under the arm	More about the way I do the job
Top of the head	Not just that it is getting done

Take a deep breath, and let it out. Say the starting statement (MPI) aloud again, "I'm expendable." Rerate the truthfulness and notice any change. If there is still a lot of emotion, consider doing the Gamut Procedure (See chapter 1) and keep tapping on this issue.

According to Native American teachings, ants can show us that we are not to build a reality based solely on our dreams. Everyone knows that ants are conscientious and hard workers. They are also expert builders. Just look at those anthills and tunnels in your ant farm. Ants can also teach us teamwork, loyalty, and how to sacrifice for the benefit of society. Notice what is going on in your life when you next see ants in unexpected places. What is the message or lesson you need to learn?

Focus on the Task

The ant can carry a leaf many miles to get back to the hill. It is a reminder to us to keep focused on the end result, even if you are going slowly or deliberately.

Say this statement aloud: "I can't focus on the task." How true does that feel on the 0–10 SUD scale? Write down your rating.

Setup (karate-chop point)— I know it is important to get the job done, to focus on the task, but sometimes it is easy to get distracted by other things. Even though I sometimes get sidetracked or lose focus on the task, I am willing for this to change. It's really bad when the task is repetitive or if I can't see progress right away. Even though this sometimes happens, I choose to refocus as soon as possible. Right now, I really need to be more task focused, and I choose to accept myself while working toward this goal.

Eyebrow	This task needs to be done
Side of the eye	It is my responsibility to get it done
Under the eye	I need to pull my own weight
Under the nose	When I get distracted
Chin	It means other people have to pick up my slack
Collarbone	Or progress toward completion gets slowed
Under the arm	I really don't want to contribute to that problem
Top of the head	This task is repetitive, over and over and over
Eyebrow	And I choose to focus on getting it done
Side of the eye	This job is pretty boring
Under the eye	And I choose to do my part anyway
Under the nose	I'm not seeing much progress
Chin	But I can persevere
Collarbone	I choose to stay focused on the goal
Under the arm	Getting this done is my goal
Top of the head	Done can be Fun!

Say the starting statement aloud again, "I can't focus on the task." Rerate the truthfulness. Feel free to continue tapping with these or similar statements if you have more work to do on the issue.

Wrapping Up

Are there times in your life when you wish you had used more ant characteristics? Tap while recalling those events. Tapping while recalling specific events is very effective. I hope you have discovered something about yourself that you might be curious to continue tapping about. If you don't have time right now, write it in your journal for later. Did an experience surface for you in which you might have been a follower and you still have some emotions about it? That would be great to tap about. The same is true for any other past experiences that involve feeling you would have benefited by being a better follower.

Did you know that there are no ants indigenous to Antarctica? Could that prompt some tapping about loneliness or feeling excluded? Ants can also lift and carry more than three times their own weight. Perhaps that might spark some future tapping on being able to handle more responsibility or setting higher goals.

One should pay attention to even the smallest crawling creatures, for these too may have a valuable lesson to teach us, and even the smallest ant may wish to communicate with a man.
—Black Elk

In the next chapter, we are going to explore some characteristics of the bat. Most people seem to have some sort of emotional reaction to bats. Take a moment before starting the next chapter to consider your gut reaction to bats and the characteristics you associate with them.

3
Chapter

Bat

I'll be perfectly honest, bats aren't my favorite animal. I'm not really afraid of them, but I am not really attracted to them either. I even considered not including them in this book, but I am very much aware that they speak to other people. My daughter-in-law actually thinks they are cute, and I have to admit that some baby bats are a little bit cute.

I think that my feelings about bats may have been influenced by the portrayal of them in many scary movies. I've never liked horror films, and bats were just lumped into that category for me. However, I was very much attracted to Batman. I grew up with the television comedy (at the time, I would have called it an action series) and even had my own Batcave that I constructed in our basement.

In several Native American traditions, such as Apache, Cherokee, and Creek, the bat is considered a trickster, much like the coyote. When speaking of a bat as a totem, there is usually a message about rebirth, ritual, and intuition. In Western culture, the bat is symbolic of the night. To get started, let's do a tapping meditation to get in touch with some of the characteristics associated with the bat.

Tapping Meditation

Eyebrow	Bat
Side of the eye	Guardian of the night
Under the eye	Bat
Under the nose	Obscurity
Chin	Bat
Collarbone	Longevity
Under the arm	Bat
Top of the head	Hypocrisy
Eyebrow	Bat
Side of the eye	Melancholy
Under the eye	Bat
Under the nose	Revenge
Chin	Bat
Collarbone	Illusion
Under the arm	Bat
Top of the head	Rebirth
Eyebrow	Bat
Side of the eye	Dreams
Under the eye	Bat
Under the nose	Intuition
Chin	Bat
Collarbone	Initiation
Under the arm	Bat
Top of the head	Journeying
Eyebrow	Bat
Side of the eye	Communication
Under the eye	Bat
Under the nose	Sleep
Chin	Bat
Collarbone	What messages do you have for me?
Under the arm	Bat
Top of the head	Open to the messages of the bat

Keep tapping while considering the knowledge, experiences, and meaning that the bat has for you. Did any of those words cause an emotional reaction for you? Be sure to write down any thoughts, beliefs, or feelings that arise.

There is a Native American legend that describes how bats came to inhabit the earth involving a little brown squirrel that was granted a wish by the sun in response to the help the squirrel gave to the sun when it got stuck. As the story goes, in the process of freeing the sun, his tail got burned off, he was blinded by the brightness of the sun, and his fur became charred or blackened. Because of the squirrel's selflessness, the sun bestowed the gifts of flight, sight in the darkness, and exceptional hearing. To me, that story puts the bat in a slightly better light.

What follows are several tapping exercises using impressions and experiences with both real bats and totem animals. I can honestly say that I have had very few real-life encounters with bats. For some reason that I don't really understand, I'd like to keep it that way. When I visited Austin, Texas, I had almost no desire to visit the bridge that is supposed to be one of the largest bat colonies. Now I'm sorry that I didn't go because I may have missed out on a great personal growth opportunity.

Prior to tapping, it might be useful for you to jot down any thoughts, feelings, or experiences that you have had related to bats. Consider that bats are associated with the night and have been called the guardians of the night. Do you have any thoughts or feelings about the night that enter your awareness when thinking about bats? If so, consider tapping about those too.

Problems Sleeping at Night

Say this statement aloud: "I can't sleep." How true does that feel on the 0–10 SUD scale? Write down your rating.

Setup (karate-chop point)—I'm having problems falling asleep. I'm having problems staying asleep too. It seems my whole sleep schedule has been turned upside down. Even though I'm having trouble sleeping at night, I choose to feel peaceful and calm. Even though it is hard for me to fall asleep at night, I choose to relax and not worry too much about it. Even though it is hard for me to stay asleep at night, I choose to trust in my body's wisdom.

Eyebrow	Can't sleep
Side of the eye	Can't sleep
Under the eye	Can't sleep at night
Under the nose	Wake up too often
Chin	Not getting enough sleep
Collarbone	So tired
Under the arm	Can't sleep
Top of the head	That is frustrating
Eyebrow	It takes too long to fall asleep
Side of the eye	Want more sleep
Under the eye	Got to have it
Under the nose	Can't sleep
Chin	This worry because I can't sleep
Collarbone	This frustration because I can't sleep
Under the arm	It is nighttime so I should be asleep
Top of the head	Can't sleep

Take a deep breath, and let it out gently. Say the starting statement (MPI) aloud again—"I can't sleep"—and rerate the intensity. What thoughts or feelings did you notice? This tapping can be a very useful tool for initiating sleep, even if we aren't talking about bats. Continue tapping for as long as feels appropriate.

Afraid of Getting Lost

What a welcome invention the GPS has been! If you have the bat as one of your totems, you probably don't get lost because you are sensitive to and aware of your surroundings, but that's not me. Getting lost used to be a general expectation. Perhaps I really needed to have the bat as one of my totems. I had a childhood friend who moved to Okeana, Ohio, a distant town, and I frequently tried to drive to visit her. I always got lost. If I took anyone with me, they would ask less-than-useful questions, such as "Does this spot look familiar?" Of course, it looked familiar. I had been lost on nearly every road in all of the surrounding towns and counties. In my own defense, it didn't help that the road signs were frequently missing. A propensity for getting lost can easily lead to feeling afraid of going to any new place.

Say this statement aloud: "I am afraid of going new places." How true does that feel on the 0–10 SUD scale or rate the intensity of the fear (10 is severe).

Setup (karate-chop point)—I have always been somewhat afraid of going new places, mostly because I'm afraid of getting lost. I don't have a very good sense of distance or direction. I'm not very spatially aware. My family has always teased me about all of my maps. In spite of this discomfort, I choose to accept who I am and how I feel. Even though I'm afraid of getting lost, I deeply and completely love and accept myself, with or without my maps. Even though I am afraid of going new places, or more specifically getting lost while going new places, I choose to relax and remain calm.

Eyebrow	Afraid of going new places
Side of the eye	Afraid of getting lost
Under the eye	Gives me a queasy stomach feeling
Under the nose	Queasiness in my stomach
Chin	About the possibility of getting lost
Collarbone	Queasiness in the middle of my stomach
Under the arm	About not knowing where I am
Top of the head	Not sure what I think would happen
Eyebrow	I've handled being lost many times in the past
Side of the eye	Sure, I've wasted some time and gas
Under the eye	But I've always been able to work it out
Under the nose	Queasy about getting lost
Chin	I choose to believe I can get to my destination safely
Collarbone	I choose to believe I can get to my destination efficiently
Under the arm	I choose to remember all of my past successes
Top of the head	I choose to believe in myself

Take a deep breath, and let it out gently. Say the problem statement again—"I am afraid of going new places"—and rerate the intensity. If there is still a lot of emotion, consider using the Gamut Procedure, and then continue tapping. If fear of getting lost is one of your demons, it might also be useful to tap about what you think might happen if you are lost. It could also help to tap while remembering specific incidents in which you were lost. Just say the story aloud while tapping on the points.

Dark Time of My Life

I'm pretty sure that everyone has a dark time in their life. If you don't have a particular affinity to bats, but you are suddenly aware of them in your daily life, there may be a message for you about a dark time that is coming or you may be in one now.

Say this statement aloud: "I'm stuck in this dark time." How true does that feel to you? Rate the feeling on the 0–10 SUD scale, with 10 being very true.

Setup (karate-chop point)—I've been going through a pretty dark time lately. I know that everyone has dark times. I don't really like how I've been feeling or even who I've been. I know I really need a change, and I choose to believe this change can happen. I don't know when. I don't know how. I'm thinking now would be a good time. Even though I've been stuck in this dark period of my life, I choose to accept who I am and how I've been feeling.

Eyebrow	This darkness
Side of the eye	Stuck in the darkness
Under the eye	This heaviness
Under the nose	Weighed down by the heaviness
Chin	The old me
Collarbone	Stuck in the darkness
Under the arm	Stuck in my cave of darkness
Top of the head	I choose to let go of the darkness
Eyebrow	I choose to be reborn into the light
Side of the eye	I relinquish old dark habits
Under the eye	And claim new habits and behaviors
Under the nose	I relinquish old dark ways of thinking
Chin	And create new patterns of thought and belief
Collarbone	I no longer need the old darkness
Under the arm	I no longer want the old darkness
Top of the head	I embrace the light as a new person

Take a deep breath, and let it out gently. Say the starting statement again: "I'm stuck in this dark time." Does it still seem true? This was a short tapping to get you started. For many people, it will take more tapping than this. You can repeat it with the words provided or perhaps you might prefer to continue tapping with your own words, thoughts, and feelings.

Gut Feelings

Have you had the experience of intuition or knowing in which there was a tiny little voice urging you to make a certain decision? Maybe you listened to it. Maybe you didn't. Bats are associated with intuition. As an animal guide, they often encourage you to follow through on your new ideas or hunches. As an animal totem, they can be associated with someone who is highly perceptive or someone who has dreams that almost always come true. For many people, putting themselves out there and acting on a new idea can be quite uncomfortable.

Say this statement aloud: "I have an uncomfortable gut feeling." How true does it feel? Don't forget to rate it on the 0–10 SUD scale.

Setup (karate-chop point)—I have this gut feeling that is really bothering me. I had a plan about what I was going to do, but my gut is telling me not to. Should I pay attention to what my gut is saying? How do I know this isn't just fear or anxiety getting in the way? Even though I have this confusion, I choose to believe I can work through this. Even though I have this confusion between my gut and my head, I choose to accept myself no matter what I decide.

Eyebrow	Gut feeling
Side of the eye	Seems like a warning
Under the eye	Could just be fear
Under the nose	Could be anxiety
Chin	Might be intuition
Collarbone	So hard to know
Under the arm	Bothersome feeling in my gut
Top of the head	Open to clarity
Eyebrow	I'd like to trust my intuition
Side of the eye	Open to clarity
Under the eye	This confusion
Under the nose	In my gut
Chin	Listening for guidance

Collarbone	Gut feeling
Under the arm	Open to clarity
Top of the head	Willing to experience the feeling

Take a deep breath, and let it out gently. Say the starting statement (MPI) again—"I have an uncomfortable gut feeling"—and rerate it. If there is still a lot of discomfort, consider using the Gamut Procedure and continue tapping until you experience relief.

Confronting My Fears

I'm sure that you have noticed that bats often have a prominent role in scary movies. When bats show up in your dreams, it can indicate that you need to address things that may be scary, such as personal fears or interpersonal frustrations. Before starting this tapping, name your fear. Consider substituting your specific fear wherever you see "this fear" in the text.

Say this statement aloud: "I am afraid." Rate the intensity of your fear on the 0–10 scale.

Setup (karate-chop point)—Confronting fears can be scary. I don't think anyone really likes doing it. Most of the time, I know it is necessary. If I don't confront it, it's just hanging there in front of me—all dark and creepy. Even though I have this fear, and I'm reluctant to confront it, I deeply and completely love and accept myself. Even though I have this fear, I choose to remember that I'm okay. Even though I have this fear, I choose to move forward to a place of confidence and love.

Eyebrow	This fear
Side of the eye	This fear
Under the eye	This fear
Under the nose	This fear
Chin	This fear
Collarbone	This fear
Under the arm	This fear
Top of the head	This fear
Eyebrow	This fear
Side of the eye	I choose to release it

Under the eye	This fear that I've always had
Under the nose	I choose to let it go
Chin	This lingering fear
Collarbone	I choose to bring it into the light
Under the arm	This fear
Top of the head	I choose to acknowledge it, accept it, and let it go

Take a deep breath, and let it out gently. Say the starting statement again, using your specific fear. Rerate the intensity. Continue tapping with the negative statements as long as necessary.

Wrapping Up

What experiences did you have during the tapping inspired by the bat? Did something come up that related to fear, gut feelings, or intuition or perhaps some dark time in your life that you have been trying for years not to think about? If so, continue tapping about those specific feelings or experiences.

For me, what came up while tapping was the need to let go of my ego. I also became more aware of my tiny little voice inside that I don't always trust but probably should. As we wrap up our tapping about bats, I wanted to share a few bat facts that might surprise you, might be a source of amusement, or may inspire more tapping. The smallest mammal is the bumble bee bat. Most bats feed on insects. Female bats usually give birth hanging upside down. Consider whether there is any trauma you need to tap on that is related to childbirth? Some bats can catch fish, and some can swim. Do you have a fear of water that keeps you from swimming? Some bats can live to be more than thirty years old, and there are no bats in Antarctica. Do you need to tap on issues related to longevity, desolation, or feeling cold?

The Bracken Bat Cave in Texas is considered to be the largest known bat colony in the world. I've seen estimates that there are more than twenty million bats there. That might be a great place to go tap if you have a phobia related to bats. Did you know that a single bat can eat more than six hundred bugs in one hour? That could inspire tapping about food consumption. In China and Japan, bats are symbols of happiness. Perhaps you could do some tapping related to happiness or lack of happiness. Most of us could benefit from that.

I hope you have learned something about bats and about yourself. In the next chapter, we will tap about bear medicine. There are many different kinds of bears, each with their own unique spirit animal twist, but for the sake of brevity, we will focus on characteristics associated with a wide variety of bears.

4 Chapter

Bear

Bears have always been special to me. I've been smitten by all kinds of bears. My earliest memory of seeing a real bear was on a trip through either Kentucky or Tennessee as a child, where there was a roadside spectacle that included a bear drinking a bottle of Coke. Also in my childhood were Smokey Bear and Gentle Ben. Later, there was Winnie the Pooh. For a while, I collected stuffed bears and continue to collect bear figurines. I have very special jewelry with images of bears or bear paws.

The bear is the first animal that I knew was a personal totem. When I meditate, I often see bears, and, as a parent, I described myself as a momma bear. When my daughter died, I was stitching a sampler that included bears. Whenever I see bears, in pretty much any form or media, I feel closer to her.

What images or feelings come into your awareness when you think about bears? Have you had experiences with bears that stand out in your memory? Join me in a tapping meditation to get in touch with some of the characteristics associated with the bear and to prepare for whatever messages the bear may have for you.

Tapping Meditation

Eyebrow	Bear
Side of the eye	Strength
Under the eye	Bear
Under the nose	Confidence
Chin	Bear
Collarbone	Leadership
Under the arm	Bear
Top of the head	Solitude
Eyebrow	Bear
Side of the eye	Quiet time
Under the eye	Bear
Under the nose	Foundation
Chin	Bear
Collarbone	Fearlessness
Under the arm	Bear
Top of the head	Healing
Eyebrow	Bear
Side of the eye	Primal power
Under the eye	Bear
Under the nose	Mothering
Chin	Bear
Collarbone	Cunning
Under the arm	Bear
Top of the head	Sovereignty
Eyebrow	Bear
Side of the eye	Gentle strength
Under the eye	Bear
Under the nose	Nurturing
Chin	Bear
Collarbone	What message do you have for me?
Under the arm	Bear

| Top of the head | Open to the message of the bear |

Did specific thoughts or feelings bubble to the surface? Were there certain characteristics you either related to or rejected? Write those down for future tapping. As we work through the exercises, I encourage you to tap through each one, even if it doesn't seem particularly relevant or intense. You never know what might come up.

Hibernation

Some bears spend their winters in hibernation. They go to sleep and avoid the cold and scarcity of winter. As winter approaches each year, I feel much less energetic and often have wished that I could hibernate. The word *hibernate* actually gives me a sense of peace and serenity that I frequently crave. It seems that I am so often bombarded with tasks, responsibilities, and requests (whether desirable or not) that the idea of hibernation is quite attractive.

Say this statement aloud: "I need to hibernate." Rate how true that is for you on the 0–10 SUD scale.

Setup (karate-chop point)—Even though I feel bombarded by all that I need or want to accomplish, I choose to feel peaceful and calm. Even though I feel stressed about all of the things going on in my world and think that hibernation would be a welcome relief, I choose to love, honor, and respect myself. Even though hibernation sometimes seems like the only way to feel less stress, I choose to allow other solutions to come gently into my awareness.

Eyebrow	I feel stressed
Side of the eye	There is so much that I want to do
Under the eye	There is so much that I feel I have to do
Under the nose	There is so much that other people want me to do
Chin	There is so much that other people say I have to do
Collarbone	And sometimes I feel like I need to get away from it all
Under the arm	I need to get away from everyone who is requesting things of me
Top of the head	I need to get away from their expectations
Eyebrow	I need to get away from my own expectations too
Side of the eye	It seems like hibernation would be a good option
Under the eye	Nobody expects bears to do anything when they are hibernating

Under the nose	I realize I have choices
Chin	About what expectations I choose to fulfill
Collarbone	And which ones I don't
Under the arm	But the consequences of saying no can feel overwhelming
Top of the head	I'm looking for a way I don't have to risk the consequences
Eyebrow	So, hibernation seems like a solution
Side of the eye	Except that I'm not a bear
Under the eye	Part of the stress comes from my own expectations and desires
Under the nose	Not from others
Chin	There are so many things I enjoy
Collarbone	And that bring me pleasure
Under the arm	And I don't like having to choose which ones I have time for
Top of the head	And which ones I don't
Eyebrow	Hibernation would take that choice away
Side of the eye	For at least part of the year
Under the eye	I remain open to other solutions
Under the nose	That would bring me more peace
Chin	I remain open to other solutions
Collarbone	That would allow me less stress
Under the arm	I am open to other solutions
Top of the head	That would increase my satisfaction in life

Take a deep breath, and let it out gently. Say the starting statement again: "I need to hibernate." Is it still very true? If your answer is yes, continue tapping with these words or switch to tapping about specific tasks, expectations, or requests that are causing you to feel stress at this particular time.

There Is Danger All Around Me

I don't think anyone would argue with the assessment that bears are quite strong. I remember an episode from the show *Gentle Ben* in which the bear actually protected the people from significant danger. When you watch the news, it becomes readily apparent that the world really can be a dangerous place, not just on TV shows. When we are feeling more vulnerable than strong, we can call upon the strength of the bear to help us cope.

Say this statement aloud: "There is danger all around me." How true does this feel to you on the 0–10 scale? If you are aware of specific dangers, use them in the tapping.

Setup (karate-chop point)—Even though there is danger all around me, I choose to remain strong in the face of adversity. Even though I see danger everywhere I look, I choose to acknowledge my inner strength. Even though there is danger in my world, I choose to exhibit fearlessness and gentle strength.

Eyebrow	I see danger all around me
Side of the eye	Danger is everywhere
Under the eye	Some of it may only be in my mind
Under the nose	But most of it is real
Chin	It makes me feel afraid
Collarbone	It makes me feel helpless
Under the arm	I don't like that feeling
Top of the head	I would rather feel strong
Eyebrow	I would rather be fearless
Side of the eye	I want to protect myself
Under the eye	I want to protect others around me if I need to
Under the nose	I wonder how that would feel?
Chin	Sure, I'd prefer that there was never anything dangerous out there
Collarbone	But that is just a fantasy
Under the arm	I can choose to respond with gentle strength
Top of the head	To both the real dangers and my inner concerns

Take a deep breath, and let it out gently. Say the problem statement again: "There is danger all around me." Is it still pretty true? If your new rating remains above a 5, consider using the Gamut Procedure, and then continue tapping.

I Worry about My Kids

At the beginning of the chapter, I mentioned that the image of the Momma Bear has always been with me. I take this one very seriously. Can you get an image in your mind of a momma bear protecting her cubs? Would you get between a bear and her cubs? That would be a very dangerous position indeed. In today's world, children are exposed to all kinds of hazards, and we can feel pretty helpless when faced with the task of protecting them.

Say this statement aloud: "I'm worried about my kids, and I am afraid I can't keep them safe." Rate the intensity of your worry on the 0–10 SUD scale.

Setup (karate-chop point)—Even though I worry about my kids, I choose to remember that I'm the Momma Bear and would do anything within my power to keep them from real harm. Even though I worry about my kids, everyone knows I've got their back. Even though I'm worried that someone might bully my kids, my mother bear instinct won't fail me.

Eyebrow	Worried about my kids
Side of the eye	Worried I won't be able to keep them safe
Under the eye	Worried they might be bullied
Under the nose	Worried they might get hurt
Chin	Worried I can't protect them
Collarbone	I'm pretty small
Under the arm	But I'm a Momma Bear
Top of the head	I'm just one person
Eyebrow	But I'm a Momma Bear
Side of the eye	I'm not usually a fighter
Under the eye	But no one gets between Momma Bear and her cubs
Under the nose	For them, I can find strength
Chin	For them, I can look larger than life
Collarbone	When I need to be, I am Momma Bear
Under the arm	I choose to act when necessary
Top of the head	I am a Momma Bear

Take a deep breath, and let it out gently. Say the starting statement aloud again, "I'm worried about my kids, and I am afraid I can't protect them. Rate the remaining emotional intensity. This is currently a hot topic in our society, and you may need to return to this and similar tapping whenever the issue presents itself. Also, bear in mind (no pun intended) that the bear might also mean the opposite for you. Perhaps you are being too much of a Momma Bear and overprotecting when the situation doesn't really call for it.

Hiding

How often do you see bears? Bear sightings in most areas are infrequent. There are always reports of bears scavenging in campgrounds, and I've occasionally seen them near dumpsters, but unlike Yogi Bear and Boo Boo, they generally stay out of sight unless they are hungry. Do you prefer to stay out of sight too? Staying out of sight can be a good thing, but it might not help you to reach your goals. The energy of the bear can help you to take this from a default mode of operation to more of a choice you make.

Say this statement aloud: "I want to hide." How true does that feel on the 0–10 SUD scale?

Setup (karate-chop point)—I have a habit of, or preference for, hiding instead of being out in the open. It feels so much safer to hide, but this hiding doesn't always bring the result I want. I don't risk rejection, but I also don't have the impact on the world that I really desire. Even though I've been hiding to stay safe, I love and accept myself. Even though I'd prefer to hide most of the time, I honor myself and my old habits. Even though I've always hidden myself behind the scenes, I am excited about the possibility of making a change, the possibility of making a difference.

Eyebrow	I like to hide
Side of the eye	I prefer to be behind the scenes
Under the eye	I dislike being out in the open
Under the nose	It is pretty scary
Chin	Too risky
Collarbone	My need to hide
Under the arm	Sure, it can keep me safe
Top of the head	But it doesn't really fit well with my goals
Eyebrow	I want to make a real difference in the world
Side of the eye	And to do that
Under the eye	I might need to stop hiding so much
Under the nose	I'd like to be more comfortable with that
Chin	I'm open to clarity about this issue
Collarbone	I choose to increase my visibility
Under the arm	And still manage to feel comfortable
Top of the head	I want to believe in my ability to protect myself, hiding or not

Take a deep breath, and let it out gently. Say the MPI statement aloud again—"I want to hide"—and rerate the truthfulness or intensity you feel. Notice any change.

Self-Knowledge Is Vital

One of the first bear characteristics mentioned in *Medicine Cards* by Jamie Sams and David Carson is the power of introspection. In Native American tradition, the Dream Lodge is a space of inner-knowing or introspection. Within the Dream Lodge, we can receive the advice of ancestors to assist in creating the future we are desiring. This is very closely associated with the power of the bear spirit. Be alert, because at times a totem or spirit animal can teach us a different lesson than we initially expect.

Are you a person who is always looking for answers outside of yourself? The bear teaches us that we have to honor our own feelings and knowledge and asks us to regain our own sense of authority. Say this statement aloud: "I am afraid to know the real me." How strong is that fear? Rate the intensity on the 0–10 SUD scale.

Setup (karate-chop point)—Knowing who I am can be terrifying. Taking a good look inside can reveal aspects of myself that I would prefer not to acknowledge. Even though I am afraid to really get to know myself, I choose to treat whatever I find with respect and dignity. Even though it is pretty scary to confront my naked self, I choose to honor the process. Even though self-knowledge is intimidating I choose to love and accept my real self, the inner me, with compassion.

Eyebrow	Self-knowledge
Side of the eye	The real me
Under the eye	My thoughts
Under the nose	My desires
Chin	My inspirations
Collarbone	How I feel about others
Under the arm	How I treat others
Top of the head	How I treat myself
Eyebrow	My beliefs
Side of the eye	My mistakes
Under the eye	My regrets

Under the nose	My secrets
Chin	My aspirations
Collarbone	What others think of me
Under the arm	What I think of me
Top of the head	Me

Take a deep breath, and let it out slowly. Say the starting statement again—"I am afraid to know the real me"—and rerate the intensity. This is a tapping exercise that often brings up a lot of emotion and can prompt a flood of old memories. You don't have to tackle them all at once. Write them down for future tapping so you don't become overwhelmed.

On Display

Looking back, I feel very bad for the poor bear that I mentioned that was in a cage, drinking Coke, and not living the life of a bear. Perhaps you have had other experiences with bears in captivity who appear miserable. I've also heard awful stories of bears being tortured to drain them of their bile and other unthinkable exploitations. On some level, can you relate to the bear that is vulnerable or on display? Say this statement aloud: "I'm on display." Is that an uncomfortable feeling for you? Rate it on the 0–10 SUD scale.

Setup (karate-chop point)—I feel like I am on display. People are watching me. I'm expected to perform. I don't like that. Even though I don't like this feeling of being on display, I choose to focus on my options. Even though I don't like feeling exposed out here on display, I choose to remain true to myself. Even though I really detest this high visibility right now, I deeply and completely love and accept myself.

Eyebrow	I'm on display
Side of the eye	This high visibility
Under the eye	Opens me up for scrutiny
Under the nose	Makes me vulnerable to judgment
Chin	They are waiting to see what I'll do
Collarbone	It even feels like they are taunting me
Under the arm	I hate being on display
Top of the head	Feeling exposed

Eyebrow	I feel vulnerable
Side of the eye	They are taunting me
Under the eye	I am exposed
Under the nose	Feels unsafe
Chin	I don't like being this visible
Collarbone	I feel judged
Under the arm	I don't think I can handle this high visibility
Top of the head	I have options
Eyebrow	Open to scrutiny
Side of the eye	I choose to remain focused
Under the eye	Possibility of judgment
Under the nose	Choosing to remain centered
Chin	High visibility
Collarbone	Choose to feel grounded
Under the arm	I accept myself and my ability to handle this situation
Top of the head	I choose to feel peaceful and calm

Take a deep breath, and let it out gently. Say the starting statement again—"I'm on display"—and rerate the intensity. Notice any changes.

Wrapping Up

Did you know that there are eight different species of bears? Only the polar bear is a true carnivore; all of the other bears are omnivores. Perhaps the bear can inspire tapping about diet issues that would assist you. Speaking of carnivores, the largest mammalian carnivore that ever lived on land was the giant short-faced bear. Does that inspire tapping about your size? Do you feel too big or too small? Another bear character I enjoy is Baloo from *The Jungle Book*. Baloo is a sloth bear. What characteristics do you think of when remembering Baloo? The most accurate way to determine a bear's age is to count the rings in a cross-section of its tooth under a microscope. Perhaps you would benefit from tapping about aging that may be inspired by the bear.

We have explored only a few of the possible ways to use the characteristics of the bear to address our own personalities and situations. What came up for you during the tapping exercises? Write it down. Meditate on it. Tap about it. Allow the spirit of the bear to help you prosper and grow.

In the next chapter, we will consider the characteristics of the deer. Do you already have some ideas about what characteristics of the deer that you might possess? You may also want to consider deer attributes that might be useful if you were to develop them more fully in your life.

5 Chapter

Deer

I've had some very interesting experiences with deer. Living in Ohio, it was very common to see deer on the side of the road, crossing the road, and dead on the road. In addition to those fairly common situations, I've had some really close encounters. While walking through my wooded backyard, I ran into a deer that hadn't quite jumped high enough to clear a fence. It had obviously been dead for quite a while, and finding such a beautiful creature in that state made me very sad. There was also the time when I was driving between my house and the grocery store when a deer ran out into the road in front of me. Don't worry; the deer was fine. I only bumped its rear end. My car was undamaged, but I was a wreck. I sat there crying, not just from the shock of it all, but because I didn't want to injure a deer. I had another experience with a deer leaping over the hood of my car when I was in my driveway. This happened very soon after hitting a deer. Clearly deer were trying to get my attention.

Deer figures can be found in Celtic, Christian, Islamic, Germanic, and Greek mythologies. The Hindu believe that the goddess Saraswati takes the form of a red deer called Rohit. Saraswati was the goddess of knowledge, music, art, wisdom, and learning. In Greek mythology, the deer is associated with Artemis, the huntress. Artemis is also the goddess of wild animals, the moon, and chastity. The deer was considered sacred to her.

Ted Andrews reminds us that the deer has often been associated with the hunt and that the hunt has led people throughout civilization and wilderness. Many mythologies tell of heroes being led to transformational experiences while chasing a deer. Deer have also figured prominently in many movies. Perhaps the most familiar is *Bambi*. I never really liked the movie and still can't watch it without crying.

Let's do a tapping meditation to get in touch with some of the characteristics associated with the deer and to get ready for whatever messages the deer might have.

Tapping Meditation

Eyebrow	Deer
Side of the eye	Highly sensitive
Under the eye	Deer
Under the nose	Strong intuition
Chin	Deer
Collarbone	Dealing with challenges gracefully
Under the arm	Deer
Top of the head	Determined
Eyebrow	Deer
Side of the eye	Gentle
Under the eye	Deer
Under the nose	Vigilance
Chin	Deer
Collarbone	Moving quickly
Under the arm	Deer
Top of the head	Innocence
Eyebrow	Deer
Side of the eye	Changing directions quickly
Under the eye	Deer
Under the nose	Gentle to self and others
Chin	Deer
Collarbone	Looking for opportunities

Under the arm	Deer
Top of the head	Kindness
Eyebrow	Deer
Side of the eye	Constantly on the move
Under the eye	Deer
Under the nose	Slow to trust
Chin	Deer
Collarbone	What message do you have for me?
Under the arm	Deer
Top of the head	Open to the messages of the deer

Keep tapping while considering the knowledge, experiences, and meaning that the deer has for you. Be sure to write down any thoughts, beliefs, or feelings that arise.

The tapping exercises that follow are based on some common traits associated with deer. In the first exercise, think about all of the different environments in which you have seen deer. At least in my experience, they seem to be everywhere.

Need to Adapt

Say this statement aloud: "I don't like change." How true does that feel to you right now? Rate the truthfulness on the 0–10 SUD scale. After you have your rating, give this brief tapping exercise a try.

Setup (karate-chop point)—I am in a position that is uncomfortable. Obviously, I don't like that. The worst part is that I can't really just walk away either. I will need to adapt. I accept myself. I may need to change a lot. I am open to eventually accepting this circumstance. I choose to learn everything necessary to manage this. Not only do I choose to adapt, but I choose to thrive.

Eyebrow	Don't like change
Side of the eye	Particularly when I'm the one who needs to change
Under the eye	Don't like change
Under the nose	Need to adapt
Chin	That's uncomfortable
Collarbone	In fact, it is downright scary
Under the arm	This need to adapt
Top of the head	Time to adapt
Eyebrow	I choose to find a way
Side of the eye	Need to adapt
Under the eye	I choose to identify my resources
Under the nose	Adaptation
Chin	I choose to focus on my goals
Collarbone	Adaptation
Under the arm	I accept myself
Top of the head	Adaptation
Eyebrow	I acknowledge the situation
Side of the eye	Adaptation
Under the eye	I acknowledge my distress
Under the nose	Adaptation
Chin	I acknowledge my choices
Collarbone	Adaptation
Under the arm	I choose to embrace the change
Top of the head	I choose to thrive

Say the problem statement aloud again: "I don't like change." Rate the new intensity. What came up for you? Was there a specific instance in which you needed to change? There likely have been many. You may want to continue tapping while focusing on one of those instances.

Gracefulness

At my current home, there are frequently deer in my backyard. Sometimes I only see one or two, and sometimes there are five or six. They are often walking around foraging, but other times, they are lying down in the shade. When I see them, I usually notice their eyes first and then the way they move. Gracefulness is one of the many qualities associated with deer medicine in Native American traditions. Close your eyes, and imagine seeing a deer stroll in front of you. What do you notice?

Say this statement aloud: "I'm not graceful. I'm a klutz." How true does that feel on the 0–10 SUD scale?

Setup (karate-chop point)—Even though I've never felt particularly graceful, I choose to accept who I am and how I feel. Even though being graceful has never been one of my gifts, I'm willing for this to change. Even though I feel pretty negative about myself because I am clumsy and not graceful, I love and accept myself.

Eyebrow	Not graceful
Side of the eye	I'm clumsy
Under the eye	Not graceful enough
Under the nose	Feeling physically awkward
Chin	Not graceful
Collarbone	I feel damaged
Under the arm	I am unable to control my body
Top of the head	I'm not graceful
Eyebrow	Not graceful
Side of the eye	I am a klutz
Under the eye	I fall over my own feet
Under the nose	I'm always banging my head on things
Chin	It's hard for me to know where my body is in space
Collarbone	I drop things all of the time
Under the arm	I'm not graceful
Top of the head	So clumsy
Eyebrow	But I'm open to change
Side of the eye	Not graceful
Under the eye	But I'm ready to improve
Under the nose	Not graceful
Chin	But I'm willing to learn

Collarbone	Not graceful
Under the arm	But I am open to changing how I move
Top of the head	I'm open to relaxing and letting my body flow

Take a deep breath, and let it out slowly. Say the starting statement (MPI) again: "I'm not graceful; I'm a klutz." If there is still a lot of emotion associated with the statement, consider using the Gamut Procedure and then repeat the tapping.

Being Gentle

It is said that gentleness can touch our hearts and minds in profound ways. When you become aware of the deer as a possible spirit animal or totem, it can be trying to tell you to find a gentleness of spirit or perhaps to stop pushing so hard to get others to change or do what you want. This desired gentleness can be physical, verbal, emotional, or spiritual. When the deer comes into your life, it can mean that you have the qualities of deer already or that you may need to develop them.

Say this statement aloud: "I'm not a gentle person." How true does that feel? Rate it on the 0–10 SUD scale.

Setup (karate-chop point)—I've never really been described as gentle. My daily persona is more like a Tasmanian devil than the gentle deer. I would like more gentleness in my life. Even though I don't think of myself as gentle, I deeply and completely love and accept myself. Even though gentle responses don't come naturally to me most of the time, I choose to believe I can adapt and change. Even though I haven't always been as gentle as I would like, I choose to accept who I am and how I respond.

Eyebrow	I value gentleness
Side of the eye	But I don't see myself as gentle
Under the eye	I want to respond more gently
Under the nose	But it doesn't come very naturally
Chin	I want to feel gentle
Collarbone	And I choose to believe that I'm just lacking a skill
Under the arm	Rather than viewing this as a character flaw

Top of the head	I want to be more gentle
Eyebrow	With others
Side of the eye	And also with myself
Under the eye	I choose to allow gentle thoughts
Under the nose	Into my life
Chin	I value gentleness
Collarbone	I choose to allow gentle actions
Under the arm	Into my life
Top of the head	I value gentleness and welcome more gentleness into my life

Take a deep breath, and let it out gently. Say the starting statement aloud again: "I'm not a gentle person." How do you feel? Take a few minutes to consider specific instances in which you would like to have been gentler and tap while describing the incidents.

Too Sensitive

If you have had the opportunity to watch a deer for any length of time, you will notice how acutely aware of their surroundings they are. Even when grazing peacefully in my yard, they have responded to every sound. In order to survive, they have developed acute senses and what I would call amazing intuition. Many people have similarly acute senses and intuition. Sometimes, it can be helpful, and other times, it seems to be uncomfortable for them. The next tapping is designed for those people with higher-level sensitivity.

Say this statement aloud: "I'm too sensitive." What kind of emotional reaction did you have? If it felt extremely negative, rate that closer to 10 on the 0–10 SUD scale. You could also remember a situation in which someone said that to you and rate the intensity you feel when recalling the event.

Setup (karate-chop point)—"You're too sensitive." That's what I have been told. Whenever I get upset by the things being said or what is going on around me, I've been blamed for being too sensitive. Being sensitive isn't a bad thing. It keeps me safe. Even though my sensitivity sometimes backfires and makes me feel worse instead of better, I love and accept all of me. Even though my sensitivity sometimes backfires and makes me feel worse instead of better, I love and accept all of me. Even though my sensitivity sometimes backfires and makes me feel worse instead of better, I love and accept all of me.

Eyebrow	I'm too sensitive
Side of the eye	That's what they say
Under the eye	I'm too sensitive
Under the nose	I'm really sick of hearing that
Chin	Too sensitive
Collarbone	Too sensitive for what?
Under the arm	Too sensitive for them?
Top of the head	Too sensitive for me?
Eyebrow	Too sensitive to be okay with rude behavior?
Side of the eye	I don't think I'm too sensitive
Under the eye	But I may want better control of my responses
Under the nose	I don't think I'm too sensitive
Chin	But I may want to change my approach
Collarbone	I am sensitive to the emotions and situations around me
Under the arm	And I don't really want that to go away
Top of the head	I choose to accept who I am, even if others don't

Take a deep breath, and let it out gently. Say the problem statement aloud again or remember the specific event and rerate your emotional reaction. This was a short tapping and very unlikely to bring full resolution if this is a hot issue. You may benefit from using the Gamut Procedure and then continuing tapping.

Wrapping Up

What other images came up for you while you were tapping about deer? I thought about innocence, the ability to listen, and understanding what is necessary for survival. Whether you noticed any qualities you share with the deer or became aware of some characteristics that may need development, be sure to write them down so that you can tap on them more in the future. You may also want to write down any memories about personal experiences with deer.

You probably already know that a male deer is called a buck, a female deer is called a doe, and a young deer is called a fawn. What I didn't know is that these labels are only true for small species of deer. In larger species, the male is called a bull, and the female is called a cow. Other names for young deer include calf and kid. When describing the red deer, the female is a hind, and the male is a hart. Do you have issues about size or gender labels that might be useful to tap about?

In the next chapter, I will introduce you to some tapping inspired by the dog. I love dogs, and that will become evident when you turn the page. The best friend quality, service to others, and unconditional love that I have experienced with dogs gives them a special place in my heart.

6

Dog

Sometimes, you choose a pet, and other times, the pet chooses you. I have had at least two occasions where the pet has chosen me.

As happens with human-dog pairings, the dog often dies before the human. I had Sigmund, a beagle mix, for fourteen years before he died, and I was not sure I could go through the pain of loving and losing another dog ever again. Having a dog as a companion in my life is as natural to me as eating and sleeping, so it wasn't very long before I decided it was time to love again.

We went to a couple of animal shelters to choose our next adoptee. My intention was set on a small, short-hair dog that didn't shed. Hah! Shadow had other plans for me. There were several puppies that met my criteria, but when they were released from their cells, they started running around, barking, wetting the floor, and generally acting crazy. My son spotted a medium-sized, long-haired dog and wanted to see her. I thought it was a bad idea because she didn't meet any of my requirements. She was cute though, and when she was let out to visit, she came quietly and sat down at our feet and waited patiently to get petted. What I now know is that she was merely allowing us to worship at her feet and was probably dehydrated, which accounted for her excellent behavior. Needless to say, she went home with us right away and died just a few weeks ago at the age of seventeen. Her loss has broken my heart into many furry pieces. Clearly, she chose us, not the other way around.

I was also chosen by Bob. Bob was a large black lab who was already advanced in age when he found me. He was walking up the street in the area of my office, and we took him in with the intention that it would only be until his owner could be located. I carefully named him Bob (from the movie *The Last Samurai*), instead of some other really cute and personal name so that I would not get too attached. Bob had other ideas. He wormed his way into my heart (which honestly did not take very long), and I was relieved that his previous owner couldn't be found and never came to claim him. Not long after, several people offered to take him since I already had two dogs, but Bob remained mine, or I his, until his death.

Now that Shadow has crossed over, I only have two dogs. Kisu is a gentle giant who also stood out from the crowd of other adorable dogs at the animal shelter. He is one of the most loving animals I have ever known and weighing more than sixty pounds, still considers himself a lapdog. His name means "kiss" in Japanese, and it fits him well. Bodhi is the newest addition to my pack. I adopted him from a mobile shelter van while I was making a routine stop at a store to get pet supplies. I saw him in the window (even though I tried hard not to look) and was initially disappointed and a bit relieved to find out that he was already claimed. I went about my business, but on the way out of the store, I noticed that he was still there. I went in and tried hard not to fall in love, but he snuggled up and fell asleep in my arms while I was petting him. I did take him home and found out later that he had a broken hip, which I'm sure is part of the reason he was so docile. Now that his hip has been repaired, he is full of energy. In their own ways, both Kisu and Bodhi came to me at times when I needed their unique love and energy.

Dogs and humans have a long history together. The stereotypes of deep loyalty, friendship, and faithfulness have proven to be true in my experience. I cannot imagine a life without dogs, and I don't even want to. My dogs have brought out the best in me, provided comfort in desolate times, made me laugh, and inspired me in so many ways.

Please join me in a meditation about the spirit of the dog. Be alert for any memories, stories, or connections that you feel.

Tapping Meditation

Eyebrow	Dog
Side of the eye	Guidance
Under the eye	Dog
Under the nose	Protection
Chin	Dog
Collarbone	Loyalty
Under the arm	Dog
Top of the head	Fidelity
Eyebrow	Dog
Side of the eye	Heroism
Under the eye	Dog
Under the nose	Watchful
Chin	Dog
Collarbone	Steadfast
Under the arm	Dog
Top of the head	Assistance
Eyebrow	Dog
Side of the eye	Intelligence
Under the eye	Dog
Under the nose	Obedience
Chin	Dog
Collarbone	Community
Under the arm	Dog
Top of the head	Family
Eyebrow	Dog
Side of the eye	Cooperation
Under the eye	Dog
Under the nose	Resourcefulness
Chin	Dog
Collarbone	What message do you have for me?
Under the arm	Dog

Top of the head   Open to the message of the dog

Keep tapping while considering the knowledge, experiences, and meaning that the dog has for you. Be sure to write down any thoughts, beliefs, or feelings that arise.

Risking Rejection

When thinking about dogs and friendships, I am struck by how differently I relate to dogs than I do to people. I don't believe I've ever felt truly rejected by a dog, but I can't say that about people. Because of that difference, I have no fear whatsoever about loving a dog. The next tapping exercise addresses the fear of rejection, a possible message from the wisdom of the dog.

Say this statement aloud: "I am afraid of rejection." How true does that feel on the 0–10 SUD scale? Remember to write down your rating.

Setup (karate-chop point)—Even though I am afraid to risk rejection ever again, I choose to at least love and accept myself. Even though it feels too risky to ever open myself up to anyone, I choose to deeply and completely love and accept myself. Even though I have been hurt pretty badly in the past when I have gotten close to others, I choose to consider the possibility that there could be a different outcome in the future.

Eyebrow   Fear of rejection
Side of the eye   Don't want to risk it
Under the eye   I need to protect myself
Under the nose   I'm not sure I could take it
Chin   If it ever happened again
Collarbone   I'm afraid to open my heart
Under the arm   I'm afraid of the heartbreak
Top of the head   Sure, my stance has its downside
Eyebrow   This fear of rejection
Side of the eye   Wanting acceptance
Under the eye   Afraid of being hurt
Under the nose   Maybe I can learn a new way
Chin   Afraid of not being loved

Collarbone	And that keeps me stuck
Under the arm	Fear of rejection
Top of the head	I choose to remain calm and loving in the face of this fear
Eyebrow	I miss out on feelings of loyalty
Side of the eye	I miss out on love
Under the eye	I miss out on commitment
Under the nose	Trying to avoid rejection
Chin	It also causes me to avoid close relationships
Collarbone	It still feels too scary to venture out there
Under the arm	But I am open to learning more about this fear
Top of the head	I am open to the possibility of feeling differently in the future

Take a deep breath, and let it out gently. Say the MPI statement again, "I am afraid of rejection." Rate the new intensity. Spend a few minutes recalling specific times and situations in which you actually felt rejected. I hope it is a short list, and you can tap about them now. If it is a long list, write them down so you can tackle them one at a time and not cause yourself too much distress. You might notice that after you have tapped on one or two specific instances, the others might not bother you very much at all.

Obedience

If you know me at all, you have probably guessed that *obedience* isn't one of my favorite words. Obedience isn't necessarily a trait some of my dogs have cultivated either. While not as independent as the stereotyped cat, my pups have often been somewhat willful, particularly in the beginning. I do expect some obedience in terms of social behavior, and in reality, dogs are known for wanting to please us. The next tapping exercise explores the concept of obedience and how it may impact our lives.

Say this statement aloud: "I hate the word *obedience*." How true does that feel? Does it bring up bad memories? Rate your emotional reaction on the 0–10 SUD scale.

Setup (karate-chop point)—Obedience. That word grates on my nerves. I don't like it at all, and I certainly don't want to apply it to myself or expectations about my own behavior. Interestingly, I don't mind applying it to others, and I certainly expected it (but usually didn't get it) from my children. This double standard deserves more attention. Even though I have an aversion to obedience for myself but expect it of others, I deeply and completely love and accept myself. Even though I have an aversion to obedience for myself but expect it of others, I deeply and completely love and accept myself. Even though I have an aversion to obedience for myself but expect it of others, I deeply and completely love and accept myself.

Eyebrow	Obedience
Side of the eye	Ugh! Even the word is bothersome
Under the eye	I instantly want to reject it
Under the nose	Obedience
Chin	Feels like being owned
Collarbone	Or being used
Under the arm	Obedience
Top of the head	There must be another way to see this
Eyebrow	How would my dog see this?
Side of the eye	Obedience
Under the eye	It feels like I have no choice
Under the nose	But I would decide who to obey
Chin	I would also choose when
Collarbone	But is that really obedience?
Under the arm	It feels very confusing
Top of the head	My dogs obey to please me
Eyebrow	My dogs obey because of trust
Side of the eye	It isn't really forced
Under the eye	Sometimes, maybe a little bit of force
Under the nose	About the required behaviors
Chin	But you can't really force the attitude
Collarbone	Obedience
Under the arm	I feel resistance at a very basic level
Top of the head	And I think lack of trust
Eyebrow	May be the real issue
Side of the eye	Obedience without trust
Under the eye	Seems like a very bad idea
Under the nose	Obedience
Chin	Not everyone can be trusted

Collarbone	I am open to more clarity
Under the arm	I am curious about my strong reactions
Top of the head	I choose to honor myself and my feelings

Take a deep breath, and let it out gently. Say the starting statement again: "I hate the word *obedience*." Rerate the emotional intensity and notice any subtle (or not so subtle) changes in the way you feel when you say it.

Obedience seems to be a complex issue, and I know that I didn't resolve it completely with the tapping. If you did, great! If not, I recommend writing down any thoughts that popped up for you. Were there specific experiences? I remembered several that required more tapping, including wedding vows.

Loyalty

Dogs are known for their loyalty. Some great examples include Hawkeye, the dog who grieved next to his Navy SEAL owner's casket, or Hachiko, the Akita who faithfully greeted his owner at the train station every day and continued to return to that same train station every day even after the owner died. Many factors likely contribute to their loyalty, including the fact that dogs are pack animals and rely upon one another for survival. They are also generally very loving creatures and somehow manage to see the best in us, whether we deserve it or not.

This tapping exercise may feel a little strange, but give it a try. This is an example of how to use tapping to gain more clarity around a complex issue, more than as an attempt for resolution about a known problem. Say this statement aloud: "I'm confused about loyalty," and rate it on the 0–10 SUD scale.

Setup (karate-chop point)—Even though I'm a little confused about loyalty, I deeply and completely love and accept myself. Even though I'm a little confused about loyalty, I choose to accept myself just as I am. Even though I'm a little confused about loyalty, I remain open to inspiration and growth.

Eyebrow	Loyalty is very important to me
Side of the eye	But I'm not sure how well I measure up
Under the eye	I think I'm loyal

Under the nose	And I can recognize times when maybe I've been too loyal
Chin	Sometimes I've stuck with a person or situation
Collarbone	Much longer than was probably reasonable
Under the arm	And I've gotten hurt
Top of the head	Or suffered in some way
Eyebrow	How can I know when to stay
Side of the eye	Or when to bail?
Under the eye	When I think about my dogs
Under the nose	I think about loyalty more as unconditional love
Chin	Always having my back
Collarbone	Would defend me to the death if need be
Under the arm	With that definition
Top of the head	Who or what am I loyal to?
Eyebrow	Certainly I'm loyal to my kids
Side of the eye	That doesn't mean I approve of everything they do
Under the eye	I don't even always like them
Under the nose	But my love is strong and forever
Chin	No matter what
Collarbone	I think it may be hard to judge loyalty
Under the arm	Particularly it if has never been tested
Top of the head	With dogs, you also think of serving a master
Eyebrow	And I don't usually think of myself as serving any master
Side of the eye	But I'm not particularly fickle or changeable in my allegiances
Under the eye	I don't exit at the first sign of disagreement
Under the nose	So, in that sense, I guess I'm pretty loyal
Chin	Sometimes, I think loyalty isn't as important
Collarbone	As maybe it once was in our society
Under the arm	As they say, change is the only constant
Top of the head	Is there a difference between change, adaptation, and loyalty?
Eyebrow	I don't know
Side of the eye	But I am open to more clarity about that
Under the eye	Although I don't have this all figured out
Under the nose	I am clear that loyalty is still very important to me

Chin	For myself
Collarbone	And I expect it from others too
Under the arm	I'm open to growth in this area
Top of the head	I aspire to the loyalty exemplified by my dogs

Take a deep breath, and let it out gently. Say the problem statement again: "I'm confused about loyalty." Rerate the truthfulness. Notice any new insights or additional questions that resulted from the tapping.

Best Friend

Most people are familiar with the assertion that a dog is man's best friend. I believe it. Frederick II, King of Prussia, is noted as having first recorded that statement when referring to one of his Italian greyhounds. Ogden Nash included a similar sentiment in one of his poems. Homer's *Odyssey* mentions that his dog, Argos, was the only one to recognize him when he returned. In 1870, George Graham Vest made closing arguments in a court case in which a man's dog named Old Drum had been shot and killed. He said, "The one absolutely unselfish friend that a man can have in this selfish world, the one that never deserts him, and the one that never proves ungrateful or treacherous is his dog." Dogs certainly have a lot to teach us about deep and lasting friendships.

Say this statement aloud: "Friendship can be difficult for me." How true does that feel on the 0–10 SUD scale? Write down your rating.

Setup (karate-chop point)—Even though I have had struggles related to making, keeping, and being a friend, I accept who I am and how I feel. Even though I have had struggles related to making, keeping, and being a friend, I accept who I am and how I feel. Even though I have had struggles related to making, keeping, and being a friend, I accept who I am and how I feel.

Eyebrow	It feels good to have friends
Side of the eye	And I've usually enjoyed having a best friend
Under the eye	But as I've grown older, that concept has changed
Under the nose	I'm not even sure what a friendship means anymore
Chin	When I was younger
Collarbone	Friendship meant someone to play with

Under the arm	And I definitely expected them to agree with pretty much everything I thought, believed, or did
Top of the head	I don't expect that anymore
Eyebrow	When I was younger, it was important to have a best friend
Side of the eye	That ensured that I would always have someone close that I could count on
Under the eye	One best friend, and maybe a few other close friends
Under the nose	That was enough for me
Chin	Now things are different
Collarbone	I have some sadness or regret about not having more friends
Under the arm	But I also don't have a lot of energy to put into making
Top of the head	Or tending to very many friendships
Eyebrow	Friendships seem more like work to me much of the time
Side of the eye	And I'm not sure why
Under the eye	I'm envious of the easy relationships
Under the nose	That other people seem to have with their friends
Chin	I'm not sure that I would make a very good "best friend" for someone else either
Collarbone	It's not that I don't want to give of myself
Under the arm	It's not that I don't care about other people
Top of the head	I definitely care
Eyebrow	But sometimes friends have really disappointed me
Side of the eye	They have let me down
Under the eye	Or done things that I just can't support
Under the nose	So, it has been easier to remain more of a loner
Chin	What does a dog have to teach me about this?
Collarbone	My dogs, or at least most of them, haven't always been glued to my side all day
Under the arm	Sometimes, they do their own thing
Top of the head	Sometimes, we cuddle
Eyebrow	Sometimes, we play
Side of the eye	But there is always the certainty of love and support

Under the eye	They know I will take care of them to the best of my ability and resources
Under the nose	And I know they would never reject me without a very good reason
Chin	But how do we know?
Collarbone	Where does that certainty come from?
Under the arm	Why are dogs better at being friends than I am?
Top of the head	I don't have all of the answers
Eyebrow	But I definitely want to know more about this
Side of the eye	While it would be inappropriate to run up to someone
Under the eye	And lick their face to say, "Hi, I'm your friend,"
Under the nose	I'm sure there are other things I can do to be friendly
Chin	I could start by just saying "hi" more often
Collarbone	Rolling over for a tummy rub would probably not be the answer
Under the arm	But asking for what I need rather than keeping it to myself might work
Top of the head	Keeping someone company on ordinary days rather than waiting for special occasions
Eyebrow	Sounds like a good first step too
Side of the eye	Making opportunities to play
Under the eye	Would probably be important
Under the nose	And never going too long
Chin	Without checking in
Collarbone	Would be pretty reassuring for both of us
Under the arm	I don't have to do friendship the way I think everyone else does it
Top of the head	But I can have satisfying friendships if I do it my way too

Take a deep breath, and let it out slowly. Say the MPI statement aloud again: "Friendship can be difficult for me." Rerate your emotional response on the 0–10 SUD scale. This was a long tapping, in part because it is usually a complex issue. For some people, relief might be instant, but for others, extra tapping may be needed. It might also be useful to do the Gamut Procedure and then continue tapping about specific friendships that might have been problematic or need tending.

Wrapping Up

Did you know that in ancient Egypt, when a pet dog died, the owner shaved off their eyebrows, smeared mud in their hair, and mourned aloud for several days? Do you need to do some tapping about the loss of one of your pets? Some other interesting facts that were new to me included dogs having sweat glands between the pads on their paws and eighteen muscles just to move their ears. The Basenji is the only dog that can't bark. Dogs' nose prints are as unique as human fingerprints. Would you benefit from tapping about not having a voice or your uniqueness as a human being?

What images, memories, or fears do you have about dogs? What did you notice during the tapping? Write it down. Meditate on it. Tap about it. We've only used a few examples to illustrate how the dog totem can help us to grow.

The next chapter uses characteristics of the dolphin to stimulate personal growth. They are known for being fun, intelligent, and graceful. Do you have some ideas about what characteristics of the dolphin you might already possess? We will also consider some dolphin attributes that might be useful if they were to be developed more fully in your life. Turn the page and dive in.

7

Chapter

Dolphin

Who doesn't think dolphins are cool? They always look like they are having so much fun. I want to have that much fun. In addition to swimming and jumping out of the water all day, they can talk. How perfect is that? Dolphins have been objects of much curiosity and investigation, and they have a significant presence in the mythology of several cultures.

In Native American tribes, particularly those living near oceans, there are many stories about dolphins helping people by carrying them to shore after a boat capsized or after a big storm. There are legends of humans transforming into dolphins and becoming the protectors of the tribe. The Chumash believe that dolphins have intentionally sacrificed themselves to provide food for the tribe, and special dolphin dances take place to honor them. Do you need to do tapping about your role as a protector or tendency to self-sacrifice?

A myth from the Amazon River tells that dolphins can shapeshift and seduce women or cause insanity, and they have almost always been characterized as magical. The first culture noted to have dolphin mythology was the Minoan people from the Mediterranean. Although they did not have a written language, there were murals on the walls of their palaces illustrating dolphin mythology. Dolphins were also associated with the Greek gods Poseidon and Aphrodite and also with Dionysus. In fact, it may have been in the mythology of Dionysus where the characterization of the dolphin as a rescuing hero was born. Byzantine and Arab sailors, as well as Chinese and European explorers, all have told tales of dolphins rescuing sailors or ships that were in trouble. Going along with this, it was considered terrible karma to harm a dolphin, and in ancient Greece, it was punishable by death.

While not all of the animals I have written about have a positive association for me, dolphins definitely do. I don't think I ever missed an episode of *Flipper* when I was a child. As we prepare for our tapping meditation, reflect on your earliest memory about dolphins. Was it a personal encounter or perhaps something on television or in the movies? When you think about dolphins, is there any anxiety, or do you feel playful and happy? I was shocked recently when someone responded with anxiety after I told of my plans to swim with dolphins. I had never even considered the possibility that a dolphin would be scary to anyone. Please join me in a meditation about the spirit of the dolphin.

Tapping Meditation

Eyebrow	Dolphin
Side of the eye	Creature of kindness
Under the eye	Dolphin
Under the nose	Plays in the sea
Chin	Dolphin
Collarbone	Intelligence
Under the arm	Dolphin
Top of the head	Transcendence
Eyebrow	Dolphin
Side of the eye	Pure of heart
Under the eye	Dolphin
Under the nose	Lives in community
Chin	Dolphin
Collarbone	Powerful and gentle
Under the arm	Dolphin
Top of the head	Savior to the weak
Eyebrow	Dolphin
Side of the eye	Symbol of harmony
Under the eye	Dolphin

Under the nose	Vibrant
Chin	Dolphin
Collarbone	Leaping for joy
Under the arm	Dolphin
Top of the head	Contentment
Eyebrow	Dolphin
Side of the eye	Friendship
Under the eye	Dolphin
Under the nose	Knows how to play
Chin	Dolphin
Collarbone	What message do you have for me?
Under the arm	Dolphin
Top of the head	Open to the message of the dolphin

Keep tapping while considering the knowledge, experiences, and meaning that the dolphin has for you. Be sure to write down any thoughts, beliefs, or feelings that arise.

I have always wanted to swim with dolphins. I almost did quite a few years ago but ended up swimming with the stingrays instead. While that was a very cool experience, my primary emotion was nervousness. I anticipated feeling joy when with the dolphins. I had another opportunity, but the timing and finances weren't quite right. Two years ago, I finally did it. We took a trip to Sea World and splurged by swimming with the dolphins and with the beluga whales. While I still would like to swim with them in a less restrictive environment, it was magical.

Why Am I Here?

In terms of legend and mythology, dolphins are associated with knowing one's purpose. When you watch them, you never get a sense of self-doubt or second guessing. I want that for myself. The next tapping addresses that big existential question of what is my purpose, or why am I here? Victor Frankl wrote a very impactful book about the human need for purpose and meaning. It was based on his experiences in Nazi concentration camps and how having a purpose played such a big part in his survival. This was also a theme in the recent book by Heather Morris, *The Tattooist of Auschwitz*. On a smaller scale, there have been multiple times in my life when I was able to endure very unpleasant situations because I knew the purpose, such as painful knee surgery. On a larger scale, believing that your life has purpose helps you to stay on course when things get tough.

Say this statement aloud: "I don't know why I am here." Rate the truthfulness of that statement on the 0–10 SUD scale.

Setup (karate-chop point)—Sometimes, it is really hard to know why I am here. What is my purpose? What am I really meant to do? This uncertainty, this not knowing, is quite uncomfortable. Even though I don't know why I am here, I choose to search for my purpose. Even though I am unsure of my purpose, I choose to create meaning in my life. Even though I am not always clear about why I am here, I choose to believe that my purpose will eventually become clearer.

Eyebrow	Who am I?
Side of the eye	Why am I here?
Under the eye	What is my purpose?
Under the nose	What is my destiny?
Chin	Am I on the right path?
Collarbone	Is this my path?
Under the arm	Who am I?
Top of the head	Unanswered questions
Eyebrow	All of this uncertainty
Side of the eye	This anxiety of not knowing
Under the eye	Who am I?
Under the nose	What is my purpose?
Chin	What is the plan?
Collarbone	Uncomfortable not knowing
Under the arm	Infinite possibilities
Top of the head	Who am I?

Take a deep breath, and let it out gently. Say the starting statement aloud: "I don't know why I am here." Notice anything that might have changed. This is a tapping where I might expect many other thoughts or questions to pop in. It was a short tapping just to get you started, but most of us (myself included) will likely need a lot more tapping to address all of the aspects of an existential question of this magnitude. Write those thoughts and questions down. I know I have said this many times, but if you are like most people, you have ignored it. We all think that if we have the insight, things will get better, and they might. However, if you use tapping along with that new insight, things can get a *lot* better. Because this has so much potential to be a life changer, we are going to do another very similar tapping exercise to encourage more progress.

I Don't Know My Purpose

Say this statement aloud: "I don't know my purpose." How true does that feel on the 0–10 SUD scale?

Setup (karate-chop point)—Even though I don't feel like I really know my purpose, the big *why* of my life, I choose to feel calm and relaxed. Even though I want to already know my life's purpose, I choose to let it unfold naturally, without fear. With or without knowing my life's purpose, I choose to believe that everything will work out splendidly.

Eyebrow	I don't know my life's purpose
Side of the eye	And I have this feeling that I *should* already know
Under the eye	When I think about that, I feel sort of sick
Under the nose	I feel it in the pit of my stomach
Chin	And then feel sure that I am either
Collarbone	Somehow very inadequate
Under the arm	Or fearful that I will miss out on some opportunity
Top of the head	That I could capitalize on
Eyebrow	If only I knew
Side of the eye	Seeking my life's purpose
Under the eye	And wanting to live congruently
Under the nose	Knowing my life's purpose
Chin	And relaxing into the future
Collarbone	Searching for it
Under the arm	Yearning for it
Top of the head	Feeling somehow incomplete
Eyebrow	If I knew
Side of the eye	I wouldn't have to keep searching

Under the eye	If I knew my life's purpose
Under the nose	I could just be
Chin	If I knew
Collarbone	Things could be different
Under the arm	Wanting to know my life's purpose
Top of the head	Seeking my life's purpose

Take a deep breath, and let it out gently. Say the MPI statement again: "I don't know my life's purpose." Rerate the truthfulness on the SUD scale.

Missing the Joy

There have been multiple times in my life when I have been too serious and life felt very stressful. I've had to relearn how to have fun. For example, quite a few years ago, I went to my first drum circle. Those really are supposed to be joyous experiences. I was extremely self-conscious about whether I was doing it right. Then after some time drumming, many of the people started dancing. Watching from the sidelines, it appeared to be an expression of their inner joy. I so desperately wanted to join in but refrained. I really didn't know how to have fun. Fast-forward a few years. I went to a wedding reception where there were people dancing. I had a blast. I had stopped worrying as much about what other people would think. My dance expressed the joy inside me.

Does the dolphin's swimming and jumping look playful to you? It does to me. My experience of adulthood is that we are all way too serious and mostly have forgotten or devalued joyful play. I don't know about you, but I want that back. The energy of the dolphin can help with that.

Say this statement aloud: "I don't have enough joy." How true does that feel on the 0–10 SUD scale? It might change from day to day, so rate how you feel about it right now. Go with your first gut reaction and don't analyze the rating too much.

Setup (karate-chop point)—I have a very strong work ethic, and that is a good thing, but it sometimes interferes with having fun. Sometimes I would like to let go and feel free, dance with joy, or sail through life with abandon. Even though I feel conflicted about work versus fun, I'm okay. Even though I feel this pull between work and play, I'm pretty proud of what

I've accomplished so far. Even though I am proud of the way I work, I choose to open myself to opportunities for joy.

Eyebrow	I want more joyful experiences
Side of the eye	But I'm afraid of being a slacker
Under the eye	Hard work has gotten me where I am
Under the nose	Goofing off would feel somewhat risky
Chin	I'm not sure what I'm afraid of
Collarbone	Maybe I'm afraid I'll like it too much
Under the arm	Maybe I'm afraid of being judged
Top of the head	In the way that I judge others
Eyebrow	When they aren't working hard
Side of the eye	I judge them when they are playing
Under the eye	I already know that I judge myself
Under the nose	When I even consider playing
Chin	I'm not sure where this attitude really came from
Collarbone	But it has a strong hold on me
Under the arm	It may not be serving me so well anymore
Top of the head	But it might have in the past
Eyebrow	I am open to more clarity
Side of the eye	I forgive anyone who taught me this
Under the eye	While forgetting to teach me to play
Under the nose	I really am missing the joy
Chin	I choose to reclaim my joy
Collarbone	I choose to keep my work ethic
Under the arm	But not at the expense of joy
Top of the head	Joy is my birthright

Take a deep breath, and let it out gently. Say the starting statement again: "I don't have enough joy." Rerate the emotional intensity. Go with how you feel, and don't overthink it. It might be fun to continue tapping while imagining, in as much vivid detail as you can, dolphins leaping into the air and playing.

Mindful of the Present

As a totem, dolphins are also associated with being in the present moment, not overly concerned about the past or the future. That may be a very useful lesson. When you are doing the dishes, are you fully involved or thinking of the next thing you need to accomplish? When you are playing with your children, are you thinking about yesterday's meeting at work and the things you wish you did or didn't say? When we live in the past or future, we miss out on the now. Use the next tapping sequence to gain more clarity about living in the present moment.

Say this statement aloud: "I'm stuck in the past." How true does it feel to you on the 0–10 SUD scale?

Setup (karate-chop point)—Sometimes it is hard to be here and now. I worry about things in the past and constantly wonder if I should have done things differently. If I'm not dwelling in the past, I'm worrying about or planning something in the future. In so doing, I forfeit my now. Even though I'm becoming aware of this tendency, I haven't been able to change it much. Even though I get stuck in the past, I choose to gently nudge myself back to now as often as it takes until it becomes a habit. Even though I worry about the future, I choose to love myself just as I am.

Eyebrow	Stuck in the past
Side of the eye	And missing out on now
Under the eye	Worried about the future
Under the nose	And missing out on now
Chin	I wonder how I might change that?
Collarbone	At least some of the time
Under the arm	I want to live in the present moment
Top of the head	And relish now
Eyebrow	I can't do that if I'm stuck in the past
Side of the eye	And I can't relish now if I'm worried about the future
Under the eye	It is time now to begin to make a change
Under the nose	I can notice the world around me
Chin	I can pay attention to my current thoughts and feelings
Collarbone	Now
Under the arm	Mindful of the present

Top of the head   Mindful of now

Take a deep breath, and let it out gently. Say the starting statement again: "I'm stuck in the past." And rate the new intensity.

Wanting to Be Rescued

There are frequent stories about dolphins rescuing people. That was often a theme of the television show *Flipper*. No one really knows why dolphins might do this. I have heard of real-life encounters in which dolphins have attacked sharks that were menacing people in the water. If we think about this with animal totems in mind, it could have meaning for us about a tendency to wait for others to rescue us from some situation or perhaps speak to someone who has a strong desire to be the hero.

There has been a lot in the media recently about the rescue stories most of us grew up with, including Cinderella and Snow White. The opposition contends that these stories teach children, particularly girls, that they need to be rescued. I personally don't have any problem with those fairy tales as long as they are presented as fairy tales and accompanied by a message of empowerment. The truth is, we all could use a helping hand at times.

The following tapping is specific to feeling helpless or like a victim who needs to be rescued.

Say this statement aloud: "I need to be rescued." How true does that feel on the 0–10 SUD scale? Before starting the tapping, take some time to recall any specific times when you felt the strong need to be rescued and subtle or not so subtle messages about being helpless or needing rescue that may have been passed down to you.

Setup (karate-chop point)—Even though I really want someone or something to rescue me, I acknowledge my own personal power. Even though I sometimes feel like I need to be rescued, I choose to love and accept myself, with or without being rescued. Even though being rescued seems like it is the only way out of this situation, I choose to increase my openness to other solutions.

Eyebrow   I was raised on rescue stories
Side of the eye   Fair damsels in distress

Under the eye	Helpless captives
Under the nose	Knights in shining armor
Chin	Brave heroes
Collarbone	Triumphant dolphins
Under the arm	There have always been others
Top of the head	Ready to rescue the victims
Eyebrow	And a lot of the time, that is what I feel like
Side of the eye	A victim
Under the eye	Waiting to be rescued
Under the nose	Helpless
Chin	But I also know
Collarbone	That is not always accurate
Under the arm	Sometimes, I just don't want to be responsible for the solution
Top of the head	Or I don't want to risk anything of myself
Eyebrow	To make the needed changes
Side of the eye	Being a victim
Under the eye	Feeling powerless
Under the nose	Waiting for rescue
Chin	Hoping that I am worth rescuing
Collarbone	Loving the idea of having a hero rescue me
Under the arm	How does that really serve me?
Top of the head	I'm pretty sure that it doesn't help me anymore
Eyebrow	It might have when I was a child
Side of the eye	And really was pretty powerless
Under the eye	It might have when I was a teenager
Under the nose	And didn't know as much about the world
Chin	As I do now
Collarbone	I wonder what it would be like to let this mental program change
Under the arm	I'm open to a new way of thinking about this
Top of the head	I may not need to be a victim anymore
Eyebrow	I may not need to be rescued
Side of the eye	At least not all of the time
Under the eye	Probably not even most of the time

Under the nose	It might be good to work in the world
Chin	In a different way
Collarbone	I choose to be open to change
Under the arm	I choose to be open to change
Top of the head	I choose to be open to change

Take a deep breath, and let it out. Say this statement aloud: "I want to be rescued." If this still feels very true for you, you may want to keep tapping about this using the script provided or using your own words. It would also be a great idea to tap while describing aloud any situations in which you really did need to be rescued. Sometimes, this type of situation can bring up intense emotions. If that happens, you may need to seek professional assistance in working through the issue.

Wrapping Up

In this chapter, we used the dolphin as inspiration for tapping about life's big existential questions of "Why am I here?" and "What is my purpose?" We also tapped about missing out on joy because we are too serious, being mindful of the present, and wanting to be rescued. Take a look back at the tapping meditation at the beginning of this chapter for other dolphin characteristics that might inspire tapping and personal growth.

There are thirty-two species of marine dolphins, four types of river dolphins, and six types of porpoises. The killer whale is actually the largest dolphin. Did you know that dolphins can't chew? That shocked me. Another interesting fact I discovered was that baby dolphins are born tail first. This allows them to be delivered without drowning. Consider that for a moment. How could that guide some tapping? I know I still have some unresolved childbirth issues.

As with the other chapters, it is my intention that you will become increasingly comfortable not only with the tapping points but also in understanding how to use tapping for personal growth. We will continue this exploration using the characteristics associated with the elk in the next chapter.

8
Chapter

Elk

In the book *Medicine Cards*, Sams and Carson tell the story of the elk outrunning a mountain lion, not because it was faster, but because of its stamina. In addition, the elk knew how to pace himself so that he could use his energy to the fullest and thereby increase his stamina.

The elk conjures many different images and reactions for me. The first one is that of a school mascot. While I was growing up, the elk was the mascot for a nearby school that was much larger and much more affluent than the school I attended. I can see that it would be a fitting choice for a mascot since elks are associated with strength, perseverance, bravery, and victory. I instead often think of snobbery, social elitism, and domination when I think about the elk. What makes this somewhat ironic is that both my mother and my closest adult friend both attended that school.

I don't believe that the elk is a totem animal for me. For the animal itself, I feel neither repelled nor strongly attracted. I do think it is a totem for my best friend. I have never seen an elk, other than one stuffed and standing in a sporting goods store, but I have tried very hard to see one. I imagine it to be an awe-inspiring experience. While driving back and forth on I-25 between Albuquerque and Denver, I saw numerous signs warning of elk, but I have always arrived at my destination disappointed because of not seeing one. I have also wondered if I might actually be keeping them away with my silent prayer that our encounter not be too up close and personal.

As we prepare to do the tapping meditation about the elk, stop to consider what your experiences, impressions, expectations, and biases are concerning this animal.

Tapping Meditation

Eyebrow	Elk
Side of the eye	Strength
Under the eye	Elk
Under the nose	Agility
Chin	Elk
Collarbone	Freedom
Under the arm	Elk
Top of the head	Power
Eyebrow	Elk
Side of the eye	Nobility
Under the eye	Elk
Under the nose	Pride
Chin	Elk
Collarbone	Majesty
Under the arm	Elk
Top of the head	Time of plenty
Eyebrow	Elk
Side of the eye	Pace yourself
Under the eye	Elk
Under the nose	Endurance
Chin	Elk
Collarbone	Strong energy
Under the arm	Elk
Top of the head	Ageless wisdom
Eyebrow	Elk
Side of the eye	Sensual passion
Under the eye	Elk
Under the nose	Perseverance

Chin	Elk
Collarbone	What message do you have for me?
Under the arm	Elk
Top of the head	Open to the messages of the elk

Keep tapping while considering the knowledge, experiences, and meaning that the elk has for you. Be sure to write down any thoughts, beliefs, or feelings that arise.

Control Freak

As a totem, elk are associated with strong energy, freedom, power, and majesty. There is a sense of control over themselves as well as others. This holds a certain appeal for me. The word *control* is often used in a negative way, such as in "control freak." Used in that way, control seems to be more like manipulation of the environment or bossing others. The need to control can often be an attempt to manage anxiety. The control exemplified by the elk is more of an internal control and a lack of anxiety. Consider the origins of any control tendencies you might have as you begin tapping with the next exercise, which focuses on the negative aspect of control.

Say this statement aloud: "I'm a control freak." How true does that feel on the 0–10 SUD scale?

Setup (karate-chop point)—Even though I have a very strong need for control, I deeply and completely love and accept myself. Even though I have a need for control over myself and my environment, I love and accept myself anyway. Even though I have this need for control, I love and accept myself, just as I am.

Eyebrow	I'm a control freak
Side of the eye	I'm a control freak
Under the eye	I'm a control freak
Under the nose	Strong need for control
Chin	Strong need for control
Collarbone	Strong need for control
Under the arm	Actually, I'm pretty good at being in control
Top of the head	Being in charge
Eyebrow	I enjoy it

Side of the eye	It doesn't seem like it is hurting anyone
Under the eye	But I do worry about what others think
Under the nose	I'm a control freak
Chin	Being in control also helps keep me safe
Collarbone	It helps me feel comfortable, and I accept this part of who I am
Under the arm	Strong need for control
Top of the head	I choose to be aware of how control affects me and how it impacts others

Take a deep breath, and let it out gently. Say the starting statement aloud again: "I am a control freak," and rerate the emotional intensity you now feel. What thoughts or feelings popped into your awareness during this exercise? Did a particular word cause you to pause or stumble? Did you have the urge to talk back or argue with any of the reminder phrases? I hope so. That would be a potential growth opportunity. You may want to also tap about incidents during which someone called you a control freak. I have tapped on lots of those. How much you tap on this might be dependent on just how much of a control freak you are. I will be tapping a lot.

I Want to Be Free

What does freedom mean to you? When you think about freedom, do you think about our flag or our military? Are the concepts of slavery or civil rights forefront in your mind when you contemplate freedom? The concept of freedom is also tied to the elk as a totem animal.

Say this statement aloud: "I don't feel free." Rate it on the 0–10 SUD scale.

Setup (karate-chop point)—Even though I feel like my freedom is compromised right now, I choose to remain peaceful and calm. Even though I feel like fighting back, I choose a spirit of peace and tranquility. Even though there are things happening to me and around me that seem to threaten my personal freedom in some way, I choose to act, not react, in a calm and effective way.

Eyebrow	I value my freedom
Side of the eye	And it feels threatened
Under the eye	I feel threatened
Under the nose	I value my freedom

Chin	Something that is important to me
Collarbone	Not just physical freedom
Under the arm	Since I know I'm not physically a captive
Top of the head	But my personal freedom
Eyebrow	To make choices that are important to me
Side of the eye	And to act in ways consistent with my values
Under the eye	The freedom to use my time
Under the nose	The way that I see fit
Chin	Freedom to express myself
Collarbone	Freedom means strength
Under the arm	Freedom means power
Top of the head	Freedom to be me

Take a deep breath, and exhale gently. Say the starting statement again: "I don't feel free." Rerate the truthfulness, and notice any change in how you feel.

Sensuality and Passion

I had a tough time writing this section and had to do some tapping about whether or not to keep it in the book. All kinds of fears bubbled to the surface about using the words *sensuality* and *passion*. It felt almost like being in the fifth grade and saying the word *sex*. I tapped about whether anyone would be offended and not want to continue reading. I tapped about some internal taboo about using the words in public. As you can see, the tapping worked.

The elk is associated with sensuality and passion, although except at mating time, they generally keep to their own gender. What follows is another tapping that is designed to increase clarity or understanding of an issue as a first step toward resolution.

Say this statement aloud: "I am uncomfortable dealing with sensuality and passion." How true does that feel to you right now? Rate the truthfulness on the 0–10 SUD scale.

Setup (karate-chop point)—Even though I'm uncomfortable saying the words, I deeply and completely love and accept myself. Even though it feels awkward to think about, talk about, or tap about this, I choose to remain comfortable and calm. I guess my discomfort means that this is an area of growth that deserves my attention, and I think I'll start just getting comfortable with the words. Even though this feels a bit scary, I choose to remember that I'm okay.

Eyebrow	Sensuality
Side of the eye	The word bothers me
Under the eye	Even though I know it's really about my senses
Under the nose	That word is also associated with sex
Chin	And talking about it
Collarbone	Makes me uncomfortable
Under the arm	Passion
Top of the head	That word bothers me too
Eyebrow	I am passionate about many things
Side of the eye	And that seems okay
Under the eye	Until I talk about passion related to sex
Under the nose	Then I feel uncomfortable
Chin	I'd like to feel more comfortable
Collarbone	With the ideas of sensuality
Under the arm	And passion
Top of the head	I'm definitely a work in progress
Eyebrow	I am open to more clarity
Side of the eye	I am open to feeling more ease
Under the eye	With these words
Under the nose	I am open to feeling more comfortable
Chin	With these concepts
Collarbone	I choose to develop a more natural way
Under the arm	Of responding to these words
Top of the head	I am open to more comfort, clarity, and ease

Take a deep breath, and let it out gently. Say the MPI statement again: "I am uncomfortable with the words *sensuality* and *passion*." Use the 0–10 scale to rerate your level of discomfort.

Pacing Myself

It is said that the elk totem teaches you how to pace yourself so that you accomplish tasks without burnout or excessive fatigue. This includes concepts such as perseverance over the long haul instead of trying to do things as quickly as possible and letting go of the need to be the first one to arrive somewhere or accomplish a task. Learning to pace ourselves can be quite a challenge. I am particularly aware of this for patients with pain issues or physical challenges. It is quite common to hear of people who try to accomplish too much on days when they feel good and then are unable to do much for several days afterward because they let themselves get too fatigued or even become injured. I am often aware of my own strong desire to be the first one to arrive or the need to get something done quickly. Pacing myself isn't an area of strength for me, and perhaps I could use more elk spirit in this domain.

Say this statement aloud: "It is hard to pace myself." How true does that feel on the 0–10 SUD scale?

Setup (karate-chop point)—Even though I find it hard to pace myself sometimes, I choose to love, honor, and respect myself. Even though I sometimes wear myself out, doing more than my body can handle, I choose to become more patient with myself in the future. Even though it often seems like it is all or nothing with me, I choose to work toward having a more even, healthy pace.

Eyebrow	Pacing myself is hard
Side of the eye	I spend so much time unable to do the things I want to do
Under the eye	That when I actually have the energy
Under the nose	I don't want to waste it
Chin	I know better than to do this
Collarbone	It always turns out the same way
Under the arm	The next day, I'm too sore
Top of the head	Too worn out
Eyebrow	Too sick
Side of the eye	To do anything
Under the eye	For one day of getting everything done that I can
Under the nose	I lose more days on the couch or in bed
Chin	I keep hoping that this time, it will be different

Collarbone	But it never is
Under the arm	I need to learn how to pace myself
Top of the head	I want to learn how to pace myself
Eyebrow	I've been told that doing a little bit each day
Side of the eye	Is better for me than doing a lot in one day
Under the eye	And nothing the next
Under the nose	I'm not sure why I can't seem to embrace that
Chin	It makes a lot of sense
Collarbone	But at the time, it seems impossible
Under the arm	It's like I'm afraid
Top of the head	That if I don't do it now
Eyebrow	I never will
Side of the eye	It's time to let go of any fear
Under the eye	That I have about this
Under the nose	Fear of not getting it done
Chin	Fear that it's now or never
Collarbone	Letting go of this irrational and counterproductive fear
Under the arm	Being open to better pacing
Top of the head	Being open to taking care of myself the best way that I can

Take a deep breath, and let it out gently. Say the problem statement aloud again: "It is hard to pace myself." What is your new SUD rating? As with some of our other topics, this one is likely to require additional tapping to get to the root of the issue. Your tapping journal can be useful to help you keep track of the journey and your progress. If you felt any increase in emotional intensity, give the Gamut Procedure a try.

Time of Plenty

Many of us live with a scarcity mentality. We are often much more focused on what we don't have rather than what we do. We also spend a great deal of time worrying about the potential for future scarcity rather than acknowledging the likelihood of future abundance. The elk is often a symbol of abundance or plenty, since they always seem to have the ability to get their needs met. Before you start tapping with the next example, spend a few minutes reflecting on your thoughts, beliefs, and habits related to scarcity and abundance in your life.

Say this statement aloud: "I have a scarcity mentality." How true does that feel on the 0–10 SUD scale?

Setup (karate-chop point)—I have a scarcity mentality. I'm not sure if it comes from my childhood, social media, or somewhere else, but I'm always afraid there won't be enough—not enough time, not enough food, not enough money, not enough love, and even not enough fun. Even though I have a scarcity mentality, I choose to believe that this can change. Even though I have a scarcity mentality and I know that probably isn't helpful for me anymore, I deeply and completely love and accept myself, and I forgive myself and anyone else who has contributed to this pattern. Even though I have had a scarcity mentality and it may have helped me in the past, I choose to let it go now.

Eyebrow	Scarcity
Side of the eye	Not a pleasant word
Under the eye	Makes me feel small
Under the nose	Makes me feel helpless
Chin	Makes me feel frightened
Collarbone	Takes away my power
Under the arm	It takes away my hope
Top of the head	Scarcity
Eyebrow	Abundance
Side of the eye	Makes me feel happy
Under the eye	Makes me feel strong
Under the nose	Makes me feel powerful
Chin	Makes me feel hopeful
Collarbone	Makes me feel confident
Under the arm	Scarcity
Top of the head	Abundance
Eyebrow	Small
Side of the eye	Strong
Under the eye	Helpless
Under the nose	Powerful
Chin	Frightened
Collarbone	Confident

Under the arm	Hopeless
Top of the head	Hopeful
Eyebrow	I get to choose
Side of the eye	Which viewpoint helps me most
Under the eye	Which viewpoint is really more accurate
Under the nose	Scarcity
Chin	Or abundance
Collarbone	Clearly an abundance viewpoint
Under the arm	Will make me more effective in the world
Top of the head	I choose abundance

Take a deep breath, and let it out gently. Say, "I have an abundance mentality." How true does that feel? Keep tapping with these statements or with your own words until you can say, "I have an abundance mentality" with significantly more confidence, and "I have a scarcity mentality" doesn't feel accurate anymore.

Wrapping Up

What did you learn about yourself while tapping using the elk totem? We have tapped about our need for control, desire for freedom, sensuality and passion, the need to pace ourselves, and a scarcity/plenty mentality. In the tapping meditation, we were also exposed to other elk totem characteristics, such as strength, agility, pride, majesty, and endurance. Did any of those bring up images, thoughts, feelings, or concerns? Be sure to tap on them.

Another name for the elk is the wapiti. It is the totem animal associated with the Long Snows Moon. It is the largest member of the deer family. Interestingly, elk seem to form bonds or associations with one another and share some responsibility for the group. They can be observed taking turns with physically demanding tasks. There are even stories of them celebrating or dancing together. Would you benefit from changing the ways in which you bond with others or how you work in groups?

Elk have very few natural enemies, and their most common predator is the human. Elk generally live in same-gender herds except during mating season. Then males gather females into harems. In some Pacific Northwest Native American tribes, the elk is considered to be the protector of women. In other tribes, the elk is associated with masculinity. What change would you like to make within your same-sex or opposite-sex relationships?

As you have practiced the tapping, I hope you have become more aware of what characteristics of the elk you have already developed as well as areas where elk energy might help you to grow. In the next chapter, we are going to keep our feet on the ground but our heads in the clouds as we explore the characteristics of the giraffe.

9
Chapter

Giraffe

I have seen a photograph of myself as a young child in which I was standing next to my aunt. We were both wearing outfits that had a large giraffe on the front. I tried to find that photo again but was unsuccessful. That photo is a reminder of what may have been the beginning of my fascination with giraffes. I think my fascination may be because the giraffe has something I have always wanted—height!

I also remember a trip to Lion Country Safari. I was fascinated watching them stroll around on that huge campus. I now know that they weren't really in the wild, but as a child, I felt that I was watching them roaming free and still remember the one that walked across the road right in front of our car. I really wanted it to bend its head down and look into our car window.

In spite of my early experiences, I don't believe that the giraffe is one of my personal totems or spirit animals; however, that doesn't mean that I can't learn much from this animal about gaining perspective, taking risks, elegance, and resourcefulness.

As we get ready for the tapping meditation, stop to consider what experiences with the giraffe you may have had. Do you need more or less of any of the traits associated with the giraffe? When you are ready, please join me in a meditation about the spirit of the giraffe.

Tapping Meditation

Eyebrow	Giraffe
Side of the eye	Stretching myself
Under the eye	Giraffe
Under the nose	Sticking my neck out
Chin	Giraffe
Collarbone	Reaching as far as I can
Under the arm	Giraffe
Top of the head	Visionary
Eyebrow	Giraffe
Side of the eye	Seeing the big picture
Under the eye	Giraffe
Under the nose	Protection
Chin	Giraffe
Collarbone	Elegance
Under the arm	Giraffe
Top of the head	Clever
Eyebrow	Giraffe
Side of the eye	Perception
Under the eye	Giraffe
Under the nose	Resourcefulness
Chin	Giraffe
Collarbone	Self-expression
Under the arm	Giraffe
Top of the head	Gentle spirit
Eyebrow	Giraffe
Side of the eye	Discernment
Under the eye	Giraffe
Under the nose	Beauty
Chin	Giraffe
Collarbone	What message do you have for me?
Under the arm	Giraffe

Top of the head   Open to the messages of the giraffe

Keep tapping while considering the knowledge, experiences, and meaning that the giraffe has for you. Be sure to write down any thoughts, beliefs, or feelings that arise.

Meddling

What is the difference between meddling, helping, and caring? It may have something to do with the intention behind it. It may also have to do with who is going to benefit. Keep these possibilities in mind as you begin the next tapping sequence. Think about the nosy neighbor peeking over the fence or the tall giraffe watching from above. How do you feel? My reaction is feeling spied upon so that they can meddle or interfere with whatever I am doing. It is definitely a negative reaction. The next tapping assumes that we are the ones doing the meddling.

Say this statement aloud: "I meddle in other people's business." How true does that feel on the 0–10 SUD scale?

Setup (karate-chop point)—I have noticed a tendency to get involved in everyone else's business. I share my opinions too freely. I offer unsolicited advice. In general, I meddle in the affairs of others. Even though I have a tendency to meddle, I am open to a new way of being. Even though I tend to meddle in other people's business, I am open to understanding more about this so I can change. Even though I often meddle in things that aren't my own, I choose to believe I can reduce this unwanted behavior.

Eyebrow	Meddling
Side of the eye	Meddling
Under the eye	Meddling
Under the nose	Meddling
Chin	Meddling
Collarbone	Meddling
Under the arm	Meddling
Top of the head	Meddling
Eyebrow	This meddling
Side of the eye	Getting too involved
Under the eye	I don't like it when people do it to me
Under the nose	But I do it too
Chin	It may just be a habit
Collarbone	Or perhaps it seems like a way I can fit in
Under the arm	Fitting in is pretty important to me
Top of the head	I want to stop meddling
Eyebrow	*Meddling* is a strongly negative word to me
Side of the eye	It has a feeling of control
Under the eye	Not cooperation
Under the nose	I am open to change
Chin	What could I substitute instead?
Collarbone	I can offer support
Under the arm	I can choose to share my opinions
Top of the head	But only when asked
Eyebrow	No more meddling
Side of the eye	No more sticking my nose in where it isn't wanted
Under the eye	No more trying to control others
Under the nose	No more meddling
Chin	I can learn to fit in in other ways
Collarbone	I have plenty of my own stuff to handle
Under the arm	I certainly don't have to be responsible for everyone else's too
Top of the head	No more meddling

Take a deep breath, and let it out gently. Now say the starting statement (MPI) again: "I meddle in other people's business." Rerate the truthfulness. Did some specific events or occurrences come to mind as you were tapping? Perhaps they were about a time when you were meddling in the affairs of others. Was there an outcome you wish you could have avoided? Perhaps you had a memory of a time when someone else meddled in your business. Was there a lesson for you? I recommend that you spend some time tapping while recalling those specific events, feelings, and lessons before proceeding to the next tapping.

Reaching for More

Think about the neck of the giraffe. Now imagine it reaching up to grab a tasty leaf hanging high above. The stretching and reaching associated with the giraffe may be physical, but the giraffe totem may also be instructing us about stretching and reaching for a goal or simply stretching ourselves beyond our comfort zone.

Say this statement aloud: "I am afraid to leave my comfort zone." How does that feel?

Setup (karate-chop point)—I have this image of the giraffe stretching and reaching with its amazingly long neck. I also have an image of myself closed safely into my comfort zone without taking any risks. In that image, I am small like a mouse, not majestic and tall like a giraffe. Most of the time, I reject the comfort zone image and urge myself to stretch beyond whatever it is that I, or others, think I can accomplish. Although I would prefer to be continually reaching for more, I love and accept the part of myself that sometimes wishes for comfort and safety instead. Even though I feel that I don't always risk enough, I love and accept myself completely. Even though sometimes I have trouble reaching, risking, or leaving my comfort zone, I deeply and completely love, accept, and honor all parts of myself and choose to allow my intuition to guide me.

Eyebrow	Feeling small
Side of the eye	But wanting to be big
Under the eye	Preferring to stay in my comfort zone
Under the nose	But also wanting to reach for more
Chin	It's true that sometimes I take risks
Collarbone	But in reality
Under the arm	It is less often than I wish

Top of the head	I like to imagine myself
Eyebrow	Sticking my neck out more often
Side of the eye	Sometimes I think about doing it
Under the eye	And sometimes I actually do it
Under the nose	And sometimes I don't act at all
Chin	I'd like to know more
Collarbone	About my choices
Under the arm	I would like to think that I am listening to my intuition
Top of the head	And that my intuition is flawlessly guiding me
Eyebrow	To take risks when appropriate
Side of the eye	And to stay in my comfort zone
Under the eye	When that is in my best interest too
Under the nose	But I suspect that it's my willingness
Chin	To listen to my intuition that really is making the difference
Collarbone	I definitely have more growth
Under the arm	Coming my way in this risk-taking thing
Top of the head	Perhaps my willingness to take a risk
Eyebrow	Or to reach for more
Side of the eye	And leave my comfort zone
Under the eye	Is somehow a product of my values and priorities
Under the nose	Actually, that makes some sense to me
Chin	Reaching for more may be much easier
Collarbone	When the goal I'm reaching for is very important to me
Under the arm	And when the goal is neutral or perhaps not really desirable
Top of the head	I hold back
Eyebrow	So, when I think about reaching for more
Side of the eye	I need to identify some things
Under the eye	That are really worth reaching for
Under the nose	Things that feel important
Chin	Things that match my values
Collarbone	Reaching for more
Under the arm	Reaching for more purpose
Top of the head	Reaching for what matters

Take a deep breath, and let it out slowly. Say the problem statement aloud again: "I'm afraid to leave my comfort zone." Rerate the emotional reaction on the 0–10 scale, and notice any change. Continue tapping with these words, or substitute your own, for as long as your intuition guides you. When you are ready, move on to the next tapping exercise.

Elegant, Not Frumpy

The giraffe is often described as majestic or elegant. Although they can be fast runners, we are perhaps most familiar with their slow, stately gait. It definitely makes me think of grace, majesty, and a regal countenance. I don't know about you, but I have rarely felt elegant or majestic. More often than not, I have felt frumpy and clumsy. Particularly when I was significantly overweight, my poorly fitting clothes added to that self-image. The next tapping sequence addresses the elegance and majesty exemplified by the giraffe—not only in terms of physical movement but also the inner qualities.

Say this statement aloud: "I feel frumpy." How true does that feel on the 0–10 scale? Don't think about it; just say the first number that pops into your head. Don't forget to write it down.

Setup (karate-chop point)—Even though I don't feel elegant or majestic, I choose to accept myself just as I am. Even though I feel the opposite of elegant—frumpy—I choose to accept myself as a work in progress and love myself wholeheartedly. Even though I would like to feel elegant or majestic more often, I choose to believe that I can change this about myself with some effort and self-love.

Eyebrow	Feeling frumpy
Side of the eye	On the inside
Under the eye	And on the outside
Under the nose	Frumpy
Chin	Not elegant
Collarbone	Not majestic
Under the arm	Definitely not regal
Top of the head	Just frumpy
Eyebrow	Not just my clothes
Side of the eye	Not just my body
Under the eye	Not the way I walk

Under the nose	And not even the way I talk
Chin	It's the way I think
Collarbone	And the way I feel
Under the arm	And my view of who I am
Top of the head	Open to change
Eyebrow	Looking for inspiration
Side of the eye	Hoping to be ready for change
Under the eye	Wanting to change from the inside out
Under the nose	But willing to fake it until I make it
Chin	Sure, my clothes have improved
Collarbone	And my body has definitely improved in many ways too
Under the arm	But my thinking hasn't kept pace
Top of the head	That seems like a good place to start
Eyebrow	When I feel frumpy
Side of the eye	I choose to use affirmations
Under the eye	To change my thinking
Under the nose	When I feel frumpy
Chin	I choose to change my posture to something majestic and regal
Collarbone	And then acknowledge the positive change I've made
Under the arm	I'm a work in progress
Top of the head	And I choose to celebrate my success

Take a deep breath, and let it out elegantly. Say the MPI statement aloud again—"I feel frumpy"—and rate the new emotional intensity.

It is likely that there are specific events that have contributed to a self-image of feeling frumpy. I can think of quite a few comments from others that helped to shape my thinking in this area. While the previous tapping may be a good start, tapping about specific memories and feelings may be necessary to completely turn this around for you.

Gaining Perspective

What do you think is different when you view the same scene from high above or on the level with it? If you answered perspective, then you are correct. As a person who is, as they say, vertically challenged, it can be difficult to get perspective in the physical sense when viewing a place or even a circumstance. Do you remember what it felt like as a child when you were seated up on an adult's shoulders? I thought it felt amazing and being up there seemed to change everything. It seemed like I could finally see. Gaining perspective when you are too close to a situation emotionally can be difficult as well. That is what you will address in the next tapping. This is another tapping that is primarily written as an attempt to gain clarity around a situation or decision but can also be quite effective in changing a situation when you feel stuck. Just jump right in without a starting statement or rating.

Setup (karate-chop point)—Even though I am right in the middle of this mess, I choose to remember that a different view might be possible. Even though I am having some difficulty looking at this situation from a different perspective, I choose to remain peaceful and calm. Even though this situation feels pretty upsetting to me from this perspective, I choose to remain peaceful and calm while trying to see it from a different angle.

Eyebrow	I'm upset
Side of the eye	And I have to admit
Under the eye	That I may be too close to the situation
Under the nose	To really judge it effectively
Chin	It feels like my current perspective
Collarbone	Is accurate
Under the arm	But I am aware
Top of the head	That my feelings aren't always accurate
Eyebrow	I do not want to be upset
Side of the eye	If it isn't necessary
Under the eye	I don't want to choose my response
Under the nose	Based on poor data
Chin	I want to consider my current perspective
Collarbone	And see if a different viewpoint
Under the arm	Might be a better option
Top of the head	A part of me wants to hold on to this perspective
Eyebrow	And wants it to be right
Side of the eye	Another part of me
Under the eye	Wants to get a bigger view

Under the nose	I choose to remain peaceful and calm
Chin	While I figure this out
Collarbone	I choose to remain peaceful and calm
Under the arm	While I look at this from another person's viewpoint
Top of the head	Even if that viewpoint disagrees with mine
Eyebrow	I choose to remain peaceful and calm
Side of the eye	And that has been difficult to do
Under the eye	Sometimes in the past
Under the nose	But I know that it is the best course of action for me
Chin	And gives me the best chance of a good outcome now
Collarbone	Considering my perspective
Under the arm	And remaining peaceful and calm
Top of the head	Considering a change in perspective

Considering another perspective doesn't always lead to a change of circumstance or a change in our decisions, but it can lead to a change in our emotional state. Did you remember specific instances in which your perspective wasn't helpful? Those would be great opportunities for additional tapping.

Is It the Best Strategy for Success?

When you think about a giraffe, do you think about cleverness? I know that I didn't. In the wild, giraffes are known for their cleverness in managing their resources. They have even learned how to approach the bitter acacia tree so that they can avoid the tree's wind-borne enzymes. In the next tapping, we will consider the ways in which we can approach our goals and challenges with a similar cleverness or use more effective strategies as well as the downside of relying solely on cleverness. Again, there is no starting statement or rating needed, just start tapping.

Setup (karate-chop point)—Even though I have this tendency to try to use cleverness or strategy to reach my goal, I deeply and completely love and accept myself. Even though I can get so involved in trying to "outsmart" my challenges or challengers that I lose sight of the real goal, I deeply and completely love and accept myself. Even though I can get pretty caught up in winning rather than looking at my true goal, I deeply and completely love and accept myself.

Eyebrow	I like to win
Side of the eye	And sometimes my desire to win
Under the eye	Blocks my ability to discern my true purpose
Under the nose	It doesn't start out that way
Chin	But I can get caught up in cleverness or winning
Collarbone	And continue with something
Under the arm	Even when there is information
Top of the head	Telling me that the end goal
Eyebrow	Is no longer desirable
Side of the eye	I tend to rely too much on strategy and cleverness
Under the eye	Instead of intuition and wisdom
Under the nose	This focus on winning at all costs
Chin	This focus on cleverness instead of wisdom
Collarbone	This focus on strategy over intuition
Under the arm	I choose to allow more wisdom to enter my life
Top of the head	I choose to be more flexible
Eyebrow	Instead of remaining rigid
Side of the eye	In pursuing a goal or challenge
Under the eye	I choose to evaluate new information
Under the nose	As it comes to me
Chin	And consider its impact on the goal
Collarbone	And the best strategy for reaching it
Under the arm	Open to new ways of doing things
Top of the head	Opening to wisdom

Take a deep breath, and let it out gently. Notice any changes that occurred.

Wrapping Up

In this chapter, we explored giraffe characteristics, including using our position or vantage point to meddle in other people's business, sticking our necks out to reach for more of what we desire, feeling frumpy, gaining perspective, and seeking the best strategy for success. Continued tapping on those topics would likely be useful to most people. If those aren't your particular issues, consider some of the other giraffe characteristics included in the tapping meditation, such as perception, beauty, and being a visionary.

I learned some interesting things about giraffes while I was researching this chapter. One of my favorite new facts is that the giraffe can clean its eyes and ears with its tongue. I guess that is made easier by the fact that their tongues can be up to twenty inches long. Did you know that a full-grown giraffe can eat over one hundred pounds of leaves and twigs each day? It is the tallest living terrestrial animal and the largest ruminant. They can run up to thirty-one miles per hour, and they only sleep about 4.6 hours a day (in captivity). Could you benefit from tapping about height, exercise, or sleep? Let the giraffe guide you.

In the next chapter, we are going to explore goat characteristics. What immediately pops into your mind? I used think of two specific incidents. One was a little annoying and the other created a moment of great tenderness. Since traveling to Alaska, I now also think of keeping watch for them on the mountains. Let's get started.

10
Chapter

Goat

I really like goats, particularly baby goats. Most, but not all, of my experiences with goats have been pleasant and fun. I've enjoyed feeding them and love watching them play with each other. In a nearby town, there was a dairy that had goats available to watch and feed. I have stacks of photographs of my boys standing by the fence, and it is fun to look back and see how much they grew (relative to the fence) between visits. One notable visit was in the spring, when new baby goats had been born. My older son stuck his hand between the slats, and the newborn goat, with umbilical cord still attached, started suckling on his finger. He joyously let everyone within earshot know that the goat was nursing on him.

I have another memory that isn't quite as pleasant involving a goat chewing on the strap of my camera when I turned my back as a young child. Another time, I was knocked over by a goat who was eager to get the food in my hand.

In the media, goats are often portrayed as greedy, cunning, or brave. Think of the Norwegian fairy tale "The Three Billy Goats Gruff." What image springs to mind? As totem animals, goats are often associated with tenacity, vitality, curiosity, faith, balance, sacrifice, and virility. When watching goats, it is easy to see many of these characteristics. As you prepare for the introductory tapping meditation, stop to consider any feelings or preconceived notions you have about goats.

Do you feel any fondness or aversion to them? Are any of their most common characteristics things that you either like or dislike about yourself?

Tapping Meditation

Eyebrow	Goat
Side of the eye	Tenacity
Under the eye	Goat
Under the nose	Diligence
Chin	Goat
Collarbone	Vitality
Under the arm	Goat
Top of the head	Fertility
Eyebrow	Goat
Side of the eye	Abundance
Under the eye	Goat
Under the nose	Lust
Chin	Goat
Collarbone	Ambition
Under the arm	Goat
Top of the head	Sacrifice
Eyebrow	Goat
Side of the eye	Exploration
Under the eye	Goat
Under the nose	Curiosity
Chin	Goat
Collarbone	Provision
Under the arm	Goat
Top of the head	Faith
Eyebrow	Goat
Side of the eye	Balance
Under the eye	Goat
Under the nose	Overcoming obstacles

Chin	Goat
Collarbone	What message do you have for me?
Under the arm	Goat
Top of the head	Open to the messages of the goat

Keep tapping while considering the knowledge, experiences, and meanings that the goat has for you. Be sure to write down any thoughts, beliefs, or feelings that arise.

Discouragement

I think it is unlikely that you've never been discouraged. It happens to me on a regular basis. What do you do when it happens? What does a goat do when it encounters a barrier or setback? Casual observation tells me they don't get discouraged. Instead, they climb over, go under, or somehow plow through to the other side. Say this statement aloud: "I feel discouraged." How true does that feel on the 0–10 SUD scale?

Setup (karate-chop point)—It is so easy to get discouraged. There always seems to be an obstacle to overcome or a barrier to knock down. Can't anything ever just be easy? Even though I am feeling weighed down with discouragement, I love and accept myself anyway. Even though this discouragement keeps popping up in my life, I deeply and completely love and accept myself. Even though I am very discouraged right now, I choose to keep pushing forward anyway.

Eyebrow	Feeling discouraged
Side of the eye	Always an obstacle
Under the eye	Constant struggle
Under the nose	Nothing feels easy
Chin	I want something to please be easy
Collarbone	It is a battle
Under the arm	Never ending problems
Top of the head	More challenges
Eyebrow	Give me a break!
Side of the eye	I know I can push through like the goat
Under the eye	I've done it before
Under the nose	I just wish I didn't have to

Chin	It is so easy to get discouraged
Collarbone	I can see my goal in front of me
Under the arm	I would like to make it easier
Top of the head	This discouragement

Take a deep breath, and let it out gently. Say the starting statement again: "I feel discouraged." Does it still feel the same? What thoughts or emotions did you notice? Were there specific situations, people, or problems that you thought about? If so, keep tapping.

Making the Sacrifice

Goats have frequently been used throughout history as a sacrificial animal, and I'm assuming it was just because of availability, but I doubt they were particularly willing subjects. In our daily lives, we are often called to sacrifice something, whether it be time, money, pleasure, sleep, or sometimes our lives. Parents often make sacrifices for their children. Do you make sacrifices willingly or do you harbor resentments for sacrifices that you have made or that have been expected of you? That is the topic of this next tapping.

Say this statement aloud: "I am uncomfortable with sacrifice." How true does it feel?

Setup (karate-chop point)—*Sacrifice* is an interesting word for me and brings up many emotions. It seems that my willingness to sacrifice my own wants, needs, or desires for some other person or situation is very conditional. I'm not sure how I feel about that. Even though I feel somewhat confused about the concept of sacrifice and how it works within me, I deeply and completely love and accept myself. Even though the concept of sacrifice makes me a bit uncomfortable, I choose to remain open and relaxed as I try to grow in this area. Even though the word *sacrifice* brings up a lot of emotion for me, I choose to believe that I am whole and worthy, just as I am.

Eyebrow	Sacrifice
Side of the eye	Exactly what does that really mean?
Under the eye	Sacrifice
Under the nose	Giving up stuff?
Chin	Sacrifice
Collarbone	Others are more important than I am?
Under the arm	Sacrifice
Top of the head	Willingly?
Eyebrow	Sacrifice
Side of the eye	Against my will?
Under the eye	Sacrifice
Under the nose	A noble goal?
Chin	Sacrifice
Collarbone	A martyr?
Under the arm	Sacrifice
Top of the head	I'm pretty sure it has to be willing for it to truly be a sacrifice
Eyebrow	But maybe I'm wrong
Side of the eye	Wanting to sacrifice
Under the eye	When it is a good cause
Under the nose	Or something that is really important to me
Chin	But not wanting to sacrifice
Collarbone	When it is unimportant to me
Under the arm	Or if it is someone else making the decision
Top of the head	Instead of leaving the decision to me
Eyebrow	Sacrifice
Side of the eye	Taking one for the team
Under the eye	Sacrifice
Under the nose	Giving of my time, talents, or energy
Chin	Sacrifice
Collarbone	Laying down my life
Under the arm	Sacrifice
Top of the head	Giving something of myself

Take a deep breath, and let it out gently. Say the MPI statement aloud again: "I am uncomfortable with sacrifice." Does it still feel true? The concept of sacrifice is a pretty big one, and it is likely to have many aspects and possibly some personal experiences that have contributed to your current thoughts and beliefs. Be sure to write down anything that came up during the tapping so that you can do more tapping work later.

Getting Curious

Goats are also known for their curiosity. I'm not necessarily looking at curiosity as a good or bad thing. As with most characteristics, it can be useful or it can further complicate your life. Do you have memories of someone saying to you, "Curiosity killed the cat"? I heard this whenever I was asking for information that someone didn't want to give me or when I was looking for something they didn't want me to find. I think it is important to remember that curiosity is also what fuels many of our best discoveries and inventions. Someone has to wonder who, what, when, where, why, or how in order to learn, grow, and invent new things. As you prepare for the next tapping, engage your curious mind and look forward to the possibilities.

Say this statement aloud: "Curiosity is bad or dangerous." How true does that feel to you on the 0–10 SUD scale?

Setup (karate-chop point)—Even though I'm not as curious about myself and my world as I used to be, I deeply and completely love and accept myself. Even though my curiosity about things seems to have faded, I choose to allow it to grow within me. Even though my curiosity has been tempered over the years, I choose to rekindle my love for knowing how the world works, and I am open to learning more about myself too.

Eyebrow	It is time to get curious
Side of the eye	It is time to discover new things
Under the eye	It is time to know how things work
Under the nose	It is time to know more about myself
Chin	It is time to open myself up
Collarbone	To the possibility of knowing more about things
Under the arm	Than I do right now
Top of the head	At least the things that are really mine to know
Eyebrow	I guess this could take the form of nosiness

112

Side of the eye	About other people's stuff
Under the eye	And I don't want to invade their privacy
Under the nose	So, while I might be curious
Chin	That would not be an action I should pursue
Collarbone	But to better understand the world around me
Under the arm	And to better understand myself
Top of the head	Seem like reasonable starting places
Eyebrow	I remember my children
Side of the eye	Were always asking why
Under the eye	Why is the sky blue?
Under the nose	Why do dogs sniff butts?
Chin	Their curiosity seemed endless
Collarbone	And it drove me nuts
Under the arm	Probably because I didn't know the answers
Top of the head	And because their timing was awful
Eyebrow	But now I see the value
Side of the eye	In wondering why
Under the eye	In contemplating how
Under the nose	And I want to bring that spirit
Chin	Back into my life
Collarbone	Feeling curious
Under the arm	Trying to make sense of things
Top of the head	Embracing the curiosity that is my birthright

Take a deep breath, and let it out gently. Say the problem statement aloud again, "Curiosity is bad or dangerous." Did you become curious about anything while you were tapping?

Tenacity

Goats don't give up easily. I loved watching the goats when they were all trying to either get up on the plank that afforded a higher vantage point or to get the pellets of food that people were feeding them. Just because it wasn't their turn was not much of a deterrent. It seemed that they just never gave up. They also didn't usually repeat the same tactic over and over. Instead, they would try many different methods to achieve the objective.

Does that describe the way you operate when trying to change something or reach a goal? Many people repeat the same strategy over and over and then are quite surprised when it doesn't work. Take a minute to reflect on your own persistence or tenacity. Do you have something you can learn from the goat?

Say this statement aloud—"I give up too easily"—and rate it on the SUD scale.

Setup (karate-chop point)—Even though I tend to give up too easily at times, I deeply and completely love and accept myself anyway. Even though I don't always stick with it, or sometimes stick with the same strategy way too long, I am open to change and growth in this area. Even though my persistence isn't quite what I might like it to be in order to reach my goals, I acknowledge that I am a work in progress and the end result hasn't been decided yet. I can become more persistent anytime I want to.

Eyebrow	Give up to easily
Side of the eye	Giving up too easily
Under the eye	Never stick with it
Under the nose	I give up if it is hard
Chin	I don't like that about myself
Collarbone	I wish I could stick with things longer
Under the arm	It feels like I just cave in
Top of the head	The minute things get tough
Eyebrow	I give up too easily
Side of the eye	But I choose to love myself anyway
Under the eye	I give up too easily
Under the nose	And I think it causes problems for me
Chin	I'm not as successful as I could be
Collarbone	If I could stick with things better
Under the arm	I tend to give up too easily
Top of the head	But this could change
Eyebrow	I tend to give up too easily
Side of the eye	But this could change

Under the eye	It is not who I am
Under the nose	It is just what I do
Chin	I can change what I do
Collarbone	Sometimes I really do give up too easily
Under the arm	But the truth is, sometimes I don't
Top of the head	I can increase one behavior and decrease the other
Eyebrow	Sometimes I give up too easily
Side of the eye	But this can change
Under the eye	I'm open to understanding
Under the nose	Why sometimes I do one thing
Chin	And other times I do something else
Collarbone	Looking forward to sticking with things that are important to me
Under the arm	And having a better chance at getting what I want
Top of the head	And achieving my goals and objectives

Take a deep breath, and let it out. Now when you say, "I give up too easily," does it still feel true? Can you rate the level of truth on the SUD rating scale? If it still feels very true to you, it would likely be beneficial for you to keep tapping using these statements or some of your own until the SUD rating is very low before moving on to the next tapping exercise.

Finding My Balance

I've always been amazed at the ability of goats to balance on a very narrow plank. At the same dairy I mentioned before, the goats would walk on long boards to get from one area to another. Even though they really seemed quite narrow, the goats remained sure-footed and stable. The ability to maintain our balance, physically and emotionally, is the topic of the next tapping exercise. Before you begin, close your eyes and visualize a goat walking on a narrow plank or climbing a mountain peak with sure-footed confidence.

Say this statement aloud: "I feel off balance." How true does it feel?

Setup (karate-chop point)—Even though I often feel off balance, I deeply and completely love and accept myself. Even though I often feel off balance, I choose to honor and respect myself while I'm working on improving this. Even though I sometimes have trouble keeping my life (and body) in balance, I love, honor, and respect myself anyway.

Eyebrow	Feeling off balance
Side of the eye	Feeling off balance
Under the eye	Feeling off balance
Under the nose	Feeling off balance
Chin	Feeling off balance
Collarbone	Feeling off balance
Under the arm	Feeling off balance
Top of the head	Feeling off balance
Eyebrow	Working to feel centered and calm
Side of the eye	Working to feel centered and calm
Under the eye	Working to feel centered and calm
Under the nose	Working to feel centered and calm
Chin	Working to feel centered and calm
Collarbone	Working to feel centered and calm
Under the arm	Working to feel centered and calm
Top of the head	Working to feel centered and calm
Eyebrow	Feeling off balance
Side of the eye	But I am working to feel centered and calm
Under the eye	Feeling off balance
Under the nose	Working to feel more centered and calm
Chin	Feeling off balance
Collarbone	Choosing to feel centered and calm
Under the arm	Feeling off balance
Top of the head	Feeling more centered and calm
Eyebrow	Less off balance
Side of the eye	More centered
Under the eye	Less off balance
Under the nose	Calmer
Chin	Allowing myself to feel centered
Collarbone	Allowing myself to feel calm

| Under the arm | Feeling more balance |
| Top of the head | Feeing centered and calm |

Take a deep breath, and let it out gently. Say the starting statement again: "I feel off balance." Notice any changes. The previous tapping was different from some of the more conversational tapping styles that I have previously demonstrated and instead was based on the pattern of Patricia Carrington's Choices method. You will notice a round of negative tapping, a round of tapping that alternates negative and positive tapping, and then finishing with a round of positive tapping.

Let's Explore

Often when I think of goats, I imagine them on the mountainside, climbing seemingly impossible rocks and ridges. We got to see some of this during our helicopter ride in Alaska. They seemed like conquering explorers. This sense of adventure or penchant for exploration is another characteristic often associated with the goat as a totem or spirit animal. In the next exercise, we are going to switch things up a little bit, and the goal will be to increase something you want more of rather than to specifically reduce a characteristic that is unwanted.

Say this statement aloud: "I want to explore new things." How does that feel on the 0–10 scale? If you are not usually adventurous, your SUD rating may be low and increase after the tapping.

Setup (karate-chop point)—Sometimes, I think it would be nice to go exploring, to search for something, or to make some important discovery. Soon after that thought, fear, lack of self-confidence, or a memory of when previous attempts went terribly wrong jump into my mind. In spite of these things that hold me back, I choose to honor and respect myself. Even though I seem to be afraid to explore my world in the ways that I think might be fun and rewarding, I choose to remember that I am a work in progress and even this could change. Even though I sometimes seem to hold myself back from adventure and exploration, I choose to forgive myself for all of the times I've been too afraid to continue the journey.

Eyebrow	I love stories of explorers
Side of the eye	I always have
Under the eye	Even when I was little
Under the nose	I admired their bravery

Chin	I admired their willingness to try
Collarbone	And I envied their successes
Under the arm	But what is a good adventure story
Top of the head	Without the setbacks, injuries, roadblocks, and peril?
Eyebrow	Those are some of the things that stop me in my tracks
Side of the eye	I like the idea of adventure
Under the eye	I like the idea of exploration
Under the nose	I like the idea of excitement
Chin	But I've been unwilling to accept the risks
Collarbone	So far I haven't been able
Under the arm	To reach a good compromise
Top of the head	Excitement and adventure along with relative comfort and safety
Eyebrow	I'm not sure what I could tolerate
Side of the eye	Right now, it doesn't seem like very much
Under the eye	But perhaps I could start small
Under the nose	I don't have to climb out on a cliff
Chin	I could just try something new
Collarbone	I don't have to travel across the world
Under the arm	I could just go someplace I don't usually go
Top of the head	I'm open to knowing more about this
Eyebrow	About the things that hold me back
Side of the eye	And the inner desire to move forward
Under the eye	I'm sure that the things holding me back are just trying to protect me
Under the nose	But maybe I don't need quite as much protection as I used to
Chin	This has been with me for a long time
Collarbone	But I am a much stronger person now
Under the arm	Than I used to be
Top of the head	This could possibly be easier than I expected

Take a deep breath, and let it out slowly. Say the starting statement again: "I want to explore new things." Rerate the truthfulness. Did the number increase a little bit?

Wrapping Up

As we wrap up our tapping about the goat, take some time to notice what changes in attitude, feeling, or behavior may have occurred. Do you feel more ready to try things than you used to? Are you more curious about the world around you? Any interest in eating tin cans? (Just kidding.)

Goats were one of the first animals tamed by humans, and baby goats can stand within minutes of being born. Perhaps the goat is prompting some tapping about getting along and co-existing or about getting up and moving. Goats also have sensitive lips and use their lips to decide what they should eat and what they should not. This sometimes makes it look like they are willing to eat anything. That can obviously jump start some tapping about diet, trying new things, and discernment. Goats burp. Perhaps we could tap about doing what comes naturally or revulsion with bodily processes.

You have been tapping along with the previous exercises and should be feeling pretty comfortable with the tapping points, SUDs ratings, and the general process. Moving forward, I'm going to assume you know to rate the intensity before and after the tapping and will write down thoughts, feelings, and experiences in your tapping journal without my prompting as frequently. I will continue to prompt you for the associated MPI.

In the next chapter, we will use the characteristics of the goose, one of my personal totem animals, to continue our exploration of tapping and totems.

11
Chapter

Goose

Hank and Rita were the two adult Canada geese that showed up outside my office building one day, hung out for a season, raised a group of little ones, and then went away. They came back the next season, raised more little ones, and stayed through that following winter. It is not all that unusual to see Canada geese throughout the entire year in Beavercreek, Ohio. Hank had an unusual mark on his neck and a pleasant personality. Sometimes, he would take food from my hand. Rita was not particularly pleasant and avoided human company at all times. When Hank was being friendly, Rita was squawking up a storm. I'm sure she was warning him about the danger of his foolish ways.

There was a pond nearby where Rita and Hank would take turns guarding a nest and nurturing their goslings. It was quite a joy to walk to the pond to observe their progress and watch the goslings take their first swims. When the goslings were a little older, Hank and Rita (she was probably reluctant) brought them up to the office building as if to show me their new kids. I was fascinated with what appeared to be a complex social structure and family life for these birds. As the couple grew into a small flock, there appeared to be a social hierarchy, delegation of work, and true affection for one another.

Unfortunately, not everyone in my building was as enamored with the geese as I was. Some would actively chase them away. Once established in the area, they were more than a little reluctant to leave, and they did make quite a mess at times in the surrounding grassy area. Geese are determined and somewhat rigid. The goose, as a totem or spirit animal, can signify a love of home, and I saw this with Hank and Rita. Our office lawn and surrounding area was home for them, and they fiercely defended it.

I can't say for sure, but I believe the owner of the office building actually shot and killed Hank and Rita for soiling his lawn. I used to worry that I had somehow contributed to their demise by being friendly with them and providing food that may have tempted them to stick around when they might have moved elsewhere if they were hungry. It is just as likely that they stayed to teach me the lessons of the goose. From them, I did recognize the importance of family and home, as well as the benefit and security of having someone who is watching your back.

Your geographic location may be a factor in your exposure to geese. Think back to the first time that you saw them flying in formation. Have you stood to admire the fuzzy little babies in the spring? Have you been chased around a parking lot by a protective female trying to keep you away from her nest? What feelings do you have when you remember those events? Write down any questions, past events, or thoughts that might be associated with geese, and then begin the tapping meditation.

Tapping Meditation

Eyebrow	Goose
Side of the eye	Guardian of the sky
Under the eye	Goose
Under the nose	Ever watchful
Chin	Goose
Collarbone	Floating on the wind
Under the arm	Goose
Top of the head	Swift
Eyebrow	Goose
Side of the eye	Happiness
Under the eye	Goose
Under the nose	Safe return
Chin	Goose

Collarbone	Lover of home
Under the arm	Goose
Top of the head	Prudent
Eyebrow	Goose
Side of the eye	Ambitious
Under the eye	Goose
Under the nose	Determined
Chin	Goose
Collarbone	Urge for freedom
Under the arm	Goose
Top of the head	Faithful even in death
Eyebrow	Goose
Side of the eye	Sociable
Under the eye	Goose
Under the nose	Perfectionism
Chin	Goose
Collarbone	What message do you have for me?
Under the arm	Goose
Top of the head	Open to the message of the goose

The goose mainly brings positive thoughts, memories, and feelings for me. I am fairly certain that this is one of my totem animals. That said, I can also relate to some goose symbolism or characteristics that might be problematic in my life.

Wanting—No, Needing—to Be Perfect

The goose is often associated with perfectionism. I'm sure I can hear those of you who know me taking an audible gasp of air. Yes, I'll admit it. I can be somewhat perfectionistic (but not about everything), and it sometimes interferes with my life. One example is this book. Part of the delay in getting it completed was my fear that there might be mistakes. Take a few moments and check in with your own perfectionistic tendencies, or lack thereof, and get started with the next tapping exercise.

MPI: "I need to be perfect." Go with your initial gut reaction when you rate it.

Setup (karate-chop point)—Even though I want to be perfect in most everything I do, or at least I want others to think that I'm perfect, I choose to love, honor, and respect myself just as I am in this moment. Even though perfectionism is something I know can be over the top, I don't want to let go of my high standards. I choose to allow myself to grow and develop in this area. In spite of my tendency to be really hard on myself and expect a standard of perfection that isn't really possible, healthy, or effective, I deeply and completely love and respect myself as a work in progress.

Eyebrow	Perfectionism
Side of the eye	An unattainable standard
Under the eye	It seems like a good goal
Under the nose	But it really seems to lower my productivity
Chin	And stifle my creativity
Collarbone	My rational brain knows that perfectionism isn't possible
Under the arm	But my emotional brain sees it as a necessity
Top of the head	This need to be perfect
Eyebrow	There seems to be a lot attached to this
Side of the eye	It almost seems necessary
Under the eye	Sure, I got lots of praise when I did things well
Under the nose	And experienced criticism if I didn't
Chin	That is normal for most people
Collarbone	But I feel that criticism very deeply
Under the arm	And I've gotten quite good at being my own critic
Top of the head	In spite of all of this
Eyebrow	I am trying to learn to love and respect myself more
Side of the eye	Perfectionism
Under the eye	A double-edged sword
Under the nose	It can help me
Chin	And it can definitely hurt me
Collarbone	The truth is
Under the arm	I feel safer if I am the one doing the criticizing
Top of the head	Rather than waiting for someone else to do it
Eyebrow	And now I just seem to expect it
Side of the eye	This is definitely something I'd like to let go of

Under the eye	The perfectionism
Under the nose	The fear of criticism
Chin	Craving praise
Collarbone	Trying to prevent the embarrassment
Under the arm	Of having someone else see a flaw
Top of the head	My problem with perfectionism

For me and for many other people, perfectionism is a deeply rooted problem, and we have many experiences that have shaped our thinking. I'm pretty sure the tapping reminded you of some of the worst ones. It did for me. When I tapped through this the first time, I remembered how my father used to explode whenever something wasn't turning out the way he wanted it to and would then take it out on others.

This would be a good time to remind you that these tapping examples are only intended to get you started. You may need to tap about each topic a bit more, including other aspects that are unique to your life experiences. I frequently have to tap for a while, do something else, and then come back to it in order to clear another aspect. This is particularly true with the experiences that go back to childhood.

The Comfort of Home

Geese are associated with home and comfort, and home really is my comfort place. There are many stories of geese braving horrid weather to return home. Now that I've moved to New Mexico, I often crave the comfort of home. As a young adult, I was given a Christmas tree ornament that was a hand-painted goose. It was an addition to the many hand-painted ornaments that came from the Barker family in Oxford, Ohio. I still have the goose ornament and have such warm feelings of home each year as I place it on the tree.

I know many people who love to be constantly running around, doing things, and spending time with large groups of people. That's not me. I am generally quite comfortable in my own home, and I work pretty hard to make it a safe and nurturing space. That's not to say that I don't like people or that I am a hermit. I do value my time at home and really need to have that safe haven. Consider your feelings about home as you begin the next tapping exercise.

MPI: "I'm uncomfortable if I leave my home."

Setup (karate-chop point)—Home is where the heart is. I have a cross-stitch of that over my door. I believe it too. Home is where my heart is. But what about those times when I'm not at home, but I'd really like to be? Is there a way for me to be more comfortable when I'm not at home? Sometimes I really have trouble leaving my safe haven to go do new things. Even though I am aware of this tendency, I choose to respect my feelings and love myself completely. Even though I am sometimes quite reluctant to go do things because I prefer to stay at home, I love and accept myself and am open to more clarity about my choices. Even though once I get home, I often don't want to leave again, I love and accept myself just as I am but welcome more balance between home and the rest of the world too.

Eyebrow	Home is my safe haven
Side of the eye	And I like it that way
Under the eye	Home is my safe haven
Under the nose	And I want to keep it that way
Chin	Home is my safe haven
Collarbone	But sometimes I really do *want* to go do things
Under the arm	And sometimes I really *need* to go do things
Top of the head	And I would like that to be easier
Eyebrow	I would like that to be more comfortable
Side of the eye	Home is my safe haven
Under the eye	And I choose to feel loved there
Under the nose	Home is my safe haven
Chin	And I choose to feel safe there
Collarbone	Home is my safe haven
Under the arm	And I choose to enjoy my time there
Top of the head	Going out can be fun too
Eyebrow	Home is my safe haven
Side of the eye	And I choose to remember that going out is fun too
Under the eye	I like most places that I go
Under the nose	Home is my safe haven
Chin	And I choose to enjoy other places that I visit
Collarbone	Home is my safe haven
Under the arm	But I can choose to enjoy myself
Top of the head	Wherever I go

Eyebrow	I can have a safe haven
Side of the eye	And I can have other experiences too
Under the eye	I just want an easier transition
Under the nose	I want a smooth transition
Chin	Between home and not home
Collarbone	Wanting a more comfortable transition
Under the arm	Between home and not home
Top of the head	And allowing it to be easy

Standing Guard

At the beginning of the chapter, I mentioned Hank and Rita and described Rita as being fairly unpleasant. In all fairness, she was just doing what comes naturally to female geese—they stand guard. One of the things that has always fascinated me about geese is how their social structure allows for the adults to share responsibility for standing guard or keeping watch over the young goslings as well as nests or sleeping adults. When their territory or members of their flock are threatened, they are really quite fierce. They don't appear overly timid or fearful, yet they do attend to safety. Sometimes humans can take this too far and become very fearful of routine aspects of life or are overly vigilant in their attentiveness to danger. That is the topic of this next tapping exercise.

When you are currently in the total freak-out mode, just start tapping. You won't need any words. Just tap until you are calmer. The words of this exercise address a general tendency to freak out.

MPI: "I'm totally freaked out."

Setup (karate-chop point)—The world seems like a pretty dangerous place. There are so many bad things happening all around. Social media is full of stories about bad things happening to good people. The news is almost exclusively about how dangerous our world is. All of this has made me afraid of just about everything. I feel so unsafe most of the time. I don't think it is very helpful for me to be afraid all of the time. I want to feel calmer and more relaxed while still being aware of potential safety issues. In spite of my high level of basic fear and insecurity, I deeply and completely love and accept myself. In spite of being on constant lookout for danger, I choose to remain appropriately relaxed and calm. In spite of my previous tendencies toward nervousness and fear, I choose to be amazed by how effortlessly I will be able to change this to a level of alertness that is more beneficial and productive.

Eyebrow	Totally freaked out
Side of the eye	Looking for danger everywhere
Under the eye	And guess what—I find it
Under the nose	I suspect that sometimes I'm making it up
Chin	But better safe than sorry, right?
Collarbone	It sure feels like that is true
Under the arm	But I'm starting to wonder if it is
Top of the head	Really necessary all of the time
Eyebrow	Is there a way to keep myself safe
Side of the eye	But not be continually freaked out?
Under the eye	This constant state of alertness
Under the nose	Really isn't helping me feel any better
Chin	It isn't stopping bad things from happening
Collarbone	And I'm not any happier this way
Under the arm	I would like to feel more relaxed and calm
Top of the head	I would like to feel more secure and calm
Eyebrow	Totally freaked out
Side of the eye	I choose to feel more relaxed instead
Under the eye	What is going on may be real
Under the nose	But I am in control of how I feel
Chin	Looking for danger
Collarbone	I choose to feel calm
Under the arm	Danger may exist
Top of the head	But I am in control of how I feel
Eyebrow	Constant state of alertness
Side of the eye	I choose to feel secure and safe
Under the eye	Challenges are definitely out there
Under the nose	But I am in control of how I feel
Chin	This feels like it might be hard
Collarbone	But I choose to consider that it really could be easy

Under the arm	Sometimes it might be hard but not always
Top of the head	I choose feelings that will benefit me in each situation

Freaking out is a complex response, involving emotions, thoughts, and physical reactions, so you may need to tap on each individually. This is another instance in which the Gamut Procedure may be useful to stop the unconscious tendency to hold on to this response to preserve safety.

Feeling Judged

One of the spirit animal messages associated with the goose is about being judgmental. I don't experience feelings of judgment or being judged when I think about geese; however, judging others and feeling judged myself is something I am very familiar with, and I know that tapping can help with these issues.

MPI: "I'm feeling judged."

Setup (karate-chop point)—Even though I'm feeling judged in this situation right now, I choose to honor who and what I am. Even though I'm feeling judged in this situation right now, I deeply and completely love and accept myself anyway. Even though I'm feeling judged in this situation right now, I choose to treat myself with love and compassion.

Eyebrow	Feeling judged
Side of the eye	And not in a good way
Under the eye	Feeling judged as unworthy
Under the nose	Or not good enough in some way
Chin	This is a feeling that always gets me
Collarbone	In the pit of my stomach
Under the arm	I feel it in my jaw
Top of the head	I feel it at the back of my neck
Eyebrow	It definitely triggers my own issues with self-worth
Side of the eye	And self-loathing
Under the eye	I thought I had conquered those feelings
Under the nose	But they come back so easily when I am judged by others
Chin	This judgment feeling in my body
Collarbone	This judgment feeling in my body

Under the arm	This judgment feeling in my body
Top of the head	This judgment feeling in my body
Eyebrow	This judgment feeling in my body
Side of the eye	This judgment feeling in my body
Under the eye	I really don't like it
Under the nose	I'm feeling judged
Chin	By others and now by myself
Collarbone	I can't do much about them
Under the arm	But I certainly could do something about me
Top of the head	That is the part I can control
Eyebrow	Feeling judged
Side of the eye	But letting go of the need to judge myself
Under the eye	Feeling judged
Under the nose	But choosing to love myself
Chin	Feeling judged
Collarbone	But choosing to let it roll right off
Under the arm	Without taking it inside my soul
Top of the head	Withstanding the judgment of others
Eyebrow	And not turning it into self-judgment
Side of the eye	Allowing the judgment feeling in the pit of my stomach to ease
Under the eye	This judgment from others
Under the nose	Allowing the tightness in my jaw to relax
Chin	This judgment
Collarbone	Allowing my neck to relax
Under the arm	Letting go of the judgment feeling
Top of the head	And learning to love myself, no matter what others think, say, or do.

Feeling judged is a big issue for many people, and we all respond in different ways. If tapping about feeling judged brought up intense feelings for you, please continue tapping until you experience relief. On the flip side, if you became aware of the ways that you are judgmental of others, I encourage you to write these down too. It would be a good area for future tapping.

This tapping also included a focus on body sensations. Whenever you are tapping on negative emotions that might be hard to fully describe, it can be very effective to focus on where you feel it in your body instead of going directly for the emotion itself.

Wrapping Up

As we wrap up this chapter inspired by the goose, consider what has changed for you in relation to goose characteristics such as perfectionism, the comfort of home, feeling freaked out, or feeling judged. Other goose characteristics you may want to include in future tapping might be resistance to change, taking things too seriously, ambition, or pessimism.

Canada geese can live ten to twenty-four years in the wild, and mated pairs may be together for up to twenty years or more. This might guide us to tap on longevity issues, personally and in relationships. Another fact is that geese can poop a lot. Estimates are that a group of fifty geese can produce 2.5 tons of poop a year. That really does sound like a lot. The first thing that popped into my mind was tapping about bodily functions. I also thought about it in terms of "waste" and thought that this goose characteristic could prompt us to tap about all of the different types of waste in our life, whether it be pollution or wasting time.

The next chapter will keep us up in the air with the hawk. Although both animals fly, they have very different totem characteristics.

12 Chapter

Hawk

The hawk is often considered the messenger of the gods. It also teaches us to be observant of our surroundings. Hawk energy can help with accessing the power to overcome a currently stressful or difficult situation. The hawk may ask us if there is a talent we have but aren't using or may assist if we are having trouble finding solutions to problems. But the biggest message from the hawk is *Pay Attention*!

In some Native American cultures, such as the Chippewa, Hopi, Menominee, Huron, Iroquois, and Pueblo, there are hawk clans, and hawks are often seen on totem poles in the Pacific Northwest. In these cultures, hawks are associated with courage and strength. They are also associated with protection from enemies. To possess hawk medicine is to have responsibility. Hawk energy bestows the ability to see the overall view of things, awareness of omens, receiving messages from spirit, and the ability to remember every detail.

Please join me in a meditation about the spirit of the hawk.

Tapping Meditation

Eyebrow	Hawk
Side of the eye	Soaring high above
Under the eye	Hawk
Under the nose	Bird of beauty
Chin	Hawk
Collarbone	Bird of strength
Under the arm	Hawk
Top of the head	Always watching
Eyebrow	Hawk
Side of the eye	Messenger of the spirit world
Under the eye	Hawk
Under the nose	Perspective
Chin	Hawk
Collarbone	Avoiding distraction
Under the arm	Hawk
Top of the head	Striking when the time is right
Eyebrow	Hawk
Side of the eye	Studying the situation
Under the eye	Hawk
Under the nose	Nobility
Chin	Hawk
Collarbone	Clarity
Under the arm	Hawk
Top of the head	Inspiration
Eyebrow	Hawk
Side of the eye	Grace and agility
Under the eye	Hawk
Under the nose	Seeking a higher truth
Chin	Hawk
Collarbone	What message do you have for me?
Under the arm	Hawk
Top of the head	Open to the message of the hawk

Keep tapping while considering the knowledge, experiences, and meaning that the hawk has for you.

I love hawks, and it always gives me a little thrill when I drive down the road and see a hawk perched on a street light or sign watching over the highway. This was quite common when I lived in Ohio. They gave the impression that they were always watching, like silent guardians, and I liked that. It felt protective to me. When you think about someone or something that is always watching, does it give you good feelings, or does it conjure something else? The next tapping will address the feeling that someone is always watching from a more negative response standpoint.

Say your starting statement: "I feel like I'm being watched."

Setup (karate-chop point)—Even though I feel like someone is always watching me, I deeply and completely love and accept myself. Even though I feel like someone is always watching me and I don't really like that feeling, I choose to remind myself that I'm okay. Even though I feel like someone is always watching me and I wish they would stop, I love and accept myself and all of my feelings about this experience.

Eyebrow	They're watching me
Side of the eye	And I don't like it
Under the eye	They're watching me
Under the nose	And I want them to stop
Chin	I don't like being watched
Collarbone	And I'm definitely not liking it right now
Under the arm	It's like they are waiting for me to make a mistake
Top of the head	And probably hoping that I will
Eyebrow	Then they can ridicule or punish me or both
Side of the eye	This feeling that I'm being watched
Under the eye	Being watched
Under the nose	This creepy feeling
Chin	Feeling watched
Collarbone	They're watching me
Under the arm	I don't like it
Top of the head	And I want it to stop

This was a very short tapping example. It is possible that your rating didn't change, but thoughts and emotions may have surfaced. Consider who or what you believe is watching you. Tap about some specific times when you felt watched. Try to remember exactly how it felt and, if possible, what you were thinking at the time. After that is firmly in your conscious awareness, switch to thinking about a hawk high up on a sign watching you. How different does that feel? Tap while comparing the two experiences.

Seeking Quiet Strength

Sometimes, it feels as though the people who shout the loudest are more successful, but I usually respect people with quiet strength more. There is generally no need for yelling, threats, or bravado. The hawk is a symbol for quiet strength.

MPI: "I am a yeller."

Setup (karate-chop point)—Even though I recognize my tendency to yell when it really isn't helpful or necessary, I love, honor, and respect myself. Even though I sometimes resort to yelling and bullying to get my way, I choose to exercise quiet strength like the hawk more often. Even though I sometimes get upset or try to control situations with an outward show of force, I choose to nurture my quiet strength.

Eyebrow	All this yelling
Side of the eye	All of the threats
Under the eye	All of the meanness
Under the nose	Just to get my way
Chin	Just to control people
Collarbone	Just to control a situation
Under the arm	I choose to back away from that
Top of the head	It doesn't really work all that well anyway
Eyebrow	And it doesn't reflect who I want to be
Side of the eye	Replacing outward force
Under the eye	With inner resolve
Under the nose	Replacing loud control
Chin	With quiet strength

Collarbone	Letting go of what doesn't really fit
Under the arm	And nurturing what it is I want more of
Top of the head	Choosing inner resolve and quiet strength

I hope specific situations popped into your mind so you can continue to tap using a real event in which quiet strength might have been a better option.

Bird's-Eye View

The hawk teaches us to be observant and to pay attention. That is difficult when we are stuck too deeply in the details. The next tapping is designed to help us get started looking at the bigger picture.

MPI: "I'm stuck in the details."

Setup (karate-chop point)—Even though I sometimes miss the big picture because I'm stuck in the details, I love and accept myself anyway. Even though it is difficult to get a better, bigger perspective on some things because I'm too close, I choose to step away from situations to get the bird's-eye view whenever I feel myself getting stuck. Even though I'm used to looking at problems from my limited view, I'm excited to consider a different perspective.

Eyebrow	This limited perspective
Side of the eye	Keeping me stuck
Under the eye	Shielding me from the bigger picture
Under the nose	Limiting my understanding
Chin	This ground-level perspective
Collarbone	It has its place
Under the arm	And I don't want to let it go
Top of the head	But it would be so much more useful
Eyebrow	When combined with the information
Side of the eye	From another perspective as well
Under the eye	I choose to be more flexible
Under the nose	In my perspective
Chin	So that my decisions can be

Collarbone	Based on more complete information
Under the arm	And I choose to view different perspectives
Top of the head	Almost effortlessly

Spiritual Awareness

I had the opportunity to spend time at the Outdoor Education Center in Yellow Springs, Ohio, when I was a child. This was a magnificent experience for a lot of reasons. I was spending time in nature, learning about the animals and plants native to my area, chasing the elusive indigo bunting, eating violets, and enjoying the freedom of not being in a traditional classroom. One of the animals that I became better acquainted with while I was there was the red-tailed hawk. What a beautiful creature. I still get a special feeling when I remember the experience, and I felt a familiar thrill when I saw one on my trip to Alaska. That feeling is what I would call a connection to Spirit. The hawk, as a totem, is known as a messenger of the spirit world and a symbol of spiritual awareness. The next tapping exercise will help you to explore your own spiritual connections.

MPI: "I don't feel connected to spiritual living."

Setup (karate-chop point)—Even though I am not as connected to the spiritual aspects of living as I would like to be, I choose to love and accept myself completely. Even though my connection to Spirit isn't quite what I would like it to be, I choose to respect the connection I have made and honor my willingness to grow in this area. Even though I tend to focus much more on body and mind than I do on spirit, I deeply and completely love, honor, and accept myself.

Eyebrow	A desire to be more connected
Side of the eye	To the spiritual aspects of life
Under the eye	It is not that I don't believe
Under the nose	Or that I'm not aware of Spirit
Chin	It's just that it isn't the realm I'm most comfortable with
Collarbone	Or as easily aware of
Under the arm	If I'm honest, it's the part that is easiest for me to ignore
Top of the head	And I don't think that is helpful
Eyebrow	This tendency to block out or ignore Spirit

Side of the eye	In my daily life
Under the eye	This tendency to block out or ignore Spirit
Under the nose	In my decision making
Chin	This tendency to block out or ignore Spirit
Collarbone	Even when I know it is important
Under the arm	And essential to balanced living
Top of the head	Connecting more easily to Spirit
Eyebrow	Considering Spirit
Side of the eye	Noticing Spirit
Under the eye	Feeling Spirit
Under the nose	Breathing Spirit
Chin	Consulting Spirit
Collarbone	Being Spirit
Under the arm	Loving Spirit
Top of the head	Spirit

Timing Is Everything

I'm sure you've heard the statement that *timing is everything*. I suspect that at least on some level, you believe it. For the hawk, timing is the difference between a full stomach and hunger. With that in mind, let's tap with this starting statement: "I tend to rush things."

Setup (karate-chop point)—Even though I have a tendency to rush things, to try to make them happen sooner rather than later, I acknowledge that sometimes there is a right time, or peak time, when the outcome would be best. I choose to love, honor, and accept myself even though I don't always act like I know the difference. Even though I have rushed and pushed for an outcome in my preferred time frame and totally messed it up in the process, I choose to forgive myself for my impatience. Even though my tendency to ignore the fact that things need to happen at the right time to have the best outcome, I deeply and completely love and accept myself.

Eyebrow	Pushing to make it happen
Side of the eye	In my desired time frame
Under the eye	Not necessarily the optimal time frame
Under the nose	My inability to wait

Chin	Or let a situation develop naturally
Collarbone	This lack of patience
Under the arm	Making it happen quickly
Top of the head	Instead of unfolding slowly
Eyebrow	Can you imagine a hawk swooping in too early
Side of the eye	Or too late
Under the eye	I bet it doesn't happen very often
Under the nose	Always judging the best time
Chin	To make a move
Collarbone	Not rushing it
Under the arm	Not waiting too long
Top of the head	Just at the right time
Eyebrow	Unable to wait
Side of the eye	Even if I know I'm rushing
Under the eye	Pushing
Under the nose	Hurrying
Chin	Rushing
Collarbone	Always *now*!
Under the arm	Not able to be patient
Top of the head	Can't wait for the right time
Eyebrow	Consider the optimal timing
Side of the eye	Let it happen with ease
Under the eye	No need to push
Under the nose	No need to rush
Chin	Honoring nature's time
Collarbone	Acting at the natural time
Under the arm	Let it be natural
Top of the head	Let it be easy

Wrapping Up

As we considered the hawk, we worked on discomfort when feeling watched, seeking quiet strength, connecting with Spirit, and flowing easily with time. These are pretty big topics, and you can probably tap with these for quite a while. Other characteristics associated with the hawk include awareness, caution, and finding inspiration. Those would be great areas of development for most of us. Don't forget to tap on specific experiences that popped into your mind.

Hawks are considered some of the most intelligent birds. They can see in the usual visible range, but they also can see in the ultraviolet spectrum and can detect polarized light and magnetic fields. Could you benefit from tapping about your ability to "see," either physically or intuitively? Let the hawk be your guide.

We are going to stay in the air for the next chapter but with a much smaller bird. What is the first thought, memory, or feeling that flits into your awareness when you think of the hummingbird? Do you think of the size, color, beak, or fast-moving wings? Have you ever seen one sitting still? Hummingbirds are said to possess the vibration of pure joy. Who wouldn't want more of that? Turn the page and learn more about the hummingbird.

13
Chapter

Hummingbird

I am always excited to see hummingbirds in my yard. I admire the beautiful colors and feel energized with the rapid beating of their wings. I have a hummingbird feeder in my yard, yet that is almost never where I see them. Instead, they are usually near my apricot trees, where it is much harder to get a sustained look at them.

The hummingbird is prominent in many cultural traditions. Their feathers can be found in love charms and often on ornamental items. While touring Acoma Pueblo in New Mexico, I spoke to an artisan who included hummingbirds on pottery, jewelry, and other items. He told me that the hummingbird brings messages from God.

According to Jamie Sams and David Carson, the hummingbird is associated with the Ghost Shirt or the Ghost Dance religion of the Oglala Lakota. The Ghost Dance is supposed to bring the return of the animals and make the white people disappear. The Mayans connect the hummingbird to the Black Sun and the Fifth World. In the creation myths, the Fifth World is the present world, remaining after the destruction of the four other cycles of creation.

Please join me in a meditation about the spirit of the hummingbird.

Tapping Meditation

Eyebrow	Hummingbird
Side of the eye	Time to enjoy life
Under the eye	Hummingbird
Under the nose	Lightness of being
Chin	Hummingbird
Collarbone	Expressing love more fully
Under the arm	Hummingbird
Top of the head	Adaptable
Eyebrow	Hummingbird
Side of the eye	Resilient
Under the eye	Hummingbird
Under the nose	Playful
Chin	Hummingbird
Collarbone	Optimistic
Under the arm	Hummingbird
Top of the head	Seeking out beauty every day
Eyebrow	Hummingbird
Side of the eye	Hope for the future
Under the eye	Hummingbird
Under the nose	Jubilation
Chin	Hummingbird
Collarbone	High energy
Under the arm	Hummingbird
Top of the head	Agility
Eyebrow	Hummingbird
Side of the eye	Messenger
Under the eye	Hummingbird
Under the nose	Seeking the sweetness of life
Chin	Hummingbird
Collarbone	What message do you have for me?
Under the arm	Hummingbird

Top of the head   Open to the message of the hummingbird

Keep tapping while considering the knowledge, experiences, and meaning that the hummingbird has for you. Be sure to write down any thoughts, beliefs, or feelings that arise.

I Can't Seem to Settle Down

It is so rare to catch a hummingbird staying still. It seems like they are always moving. That sense of constant motion is the theme for this tapping.

MPI: "I'm constantly moving."

Setup (karate-chop point)—Even though I flit from one thing to another, I honor and respect my true nature. Even though I can't seem to settle down and I just flit from one thing to another, I love and accept myself anyway. Even though I just keep moving all of the time and can't seem to rest for very long, I choose to see myself with love and clarity.

Eyebrow   I'm constantly moving
Side of the eye   I go from one thing to another like the hummingbird
Under the eye   All day long
Under the nose   It feels uncomfortable to stop
Chin   For me, it's go, go, go
Collarbone   And most of the time, it actually feels pretty good
Under the arm   But sometimes it doesn't feel good
Top of the head   Other people criticize me
Eyebrow   Those are the sitters, sleepers, and slugs
Side of the eye   They don't understand my constant activity
Under the eye   I just have so much energy
Under the nose   It is fun to be alive
Chin   There is so much to see and do
Collarbone   I could listen to what everyone else is saying
Under the arm   And try to sit still
Top of the head   But that just wouldn't be me.

I'm Just a Pessimist

The hummingbird is associated with the feeling that life is wonderful and brings joy to others. This spirit would be incompatible with pessimism, the topic of the next tapping exercise. Say the starting statement: "I am a pessimist." Be sure to give your first response when trying to rate the truth of this.

Setup (karate-chop point)—Even though I think I'm probably a pessimist, I would like to be open to a change. Even though I think I'm almost certainly a pessimist, I might be willing to consider some other options. Even though I'm pretty sure I'm a pessimist, I choose to consider optimism as a viable option in some situations.

Eyebrow	I'm a pessimist
Side of the eye	I've always been a pessimist
Under the eye	That is just my personality
Under the nose	If I'm honest, I've always been a little jealous of the optimist-types
Chin	They fly around with hope
Collarbone	With joy
Under the arm	And with expectation for each day
Top of the head	I guess I have expectations too
Eyebrow	They just aren't all that appealing
Side of the eye	Pessimism is familiar
Under the eye	But it doesn't sound like it is fitting me as well as it used to
Under the nose	I would be open to considering a change of view
Chin	I wonder what my life would be like?
Collarbone	If I were more optimistic sometimes
Under the arm	I wonder what would happen
Top of the head	If I expected good things to come my way

This tapping was just to get you started. Keep tapping with these or similar statements until you feel you have made a shift in your perspective.

Cultivating a Joyful Heart

I like to think that I have a joyful heart, and most of the time, I probably do. That said, I can easily sink into sorrow. Once I do sink, it can be hard to pull myself back up and feel the joy again. I'd like that to be an easier process. Would you? Can you imagine having the joyful heart that is associated with the hummingbird? I can. Let's tap.

MPI: "My heart is not joyful."

Setup (karate-chop point)—Even though I sometimes sink into sorrow, when what I really want is a joyful heart, I choose to treat myself lovingly when this happens instead of shaming myself. Even though I sometimes don't feel the joyful heart that I really long to have, I choose to treat myself lovingly and acknowledge that I am having a temporary experience. Even though returning to joy after feeling a bit down can take some time, I choose to be accepting of myself, no matter what.

Eyebrow	Choosing a joyful heart
Side of the eye	Isn't always as easy as I would like it to be
Under the eye	I want more joy
Under the nose	And less sorrow and sadness
Chin	At the very least
Collarbone	I want to return to joy more easily
Under the arm	Without shaming myself for feeling the sadness
Top of the head	I want to experience the lightness and freedom
Eyebrow	Of a joyful heart much more often
Side of the eye	And appreciate it more
Under the eye	When I feel joyful
Under the nose	Rather than taking it for granted
Chin	When sad things happen
Collarbone	I want to acknowledge them and feel the sadness
Under the arm	Without letting go of a naturally joyful spirit
Top of the head	Obviously, I don't want to go chirping about
Eyebrow	In an insensitive way that hurts other people
Side of the eye	I believe I am capable of feeling sad in an appropriate way
Under the eye	Without letting go of an innate sense of joy and wonder

Under the nose	No matter what life throws at me
Chin	I choose to cherish a joyful heart
Collarbone	No matter how low my mood is in the moment
Under the arm	I choose to remember that joy is my birthright
Top of the head	Choosing a joyful heart

This tapping wasn't specific to a situation but could be even more powerful if you include things that make it personal for you. Perhaps there was a specific situation or time in your life in which your joyful heart was squashed and you had trouble climbing out of the dark hole. By describing that event in detail while you are tapping and then returning to the exercise about seeking the joyful heart, you may experience a dramatic shift.

My Energy Is Low

Do you ever feel like your energy is low? Sometimes, it just seems like I'm moving in slow motion or trying to walk uphill backward. That is quite the contrast to the seemingly boundless energy of the hummingbird. Before you protest that tapping can't help with that because it is a physical problem, I want you to consider a couple of possibilities. First, tapping can definitely help with physical issues. Second, it is very difficult to discern whether there is also an emotional component when someone experiences the physical manifestations of low energy. They aren't separate systems. So, please do your best to keep an open mind and give it a try.

MPI: "My energy is low."

Setup (karate-chop point)—Even though my energy is low, and I'm pretty sure it must be a physical thing, I deeply and completely love and accept myself and am open to experiencing a positive change. Even though my energy is low, and I believe it is completely a physical problem, I'm open to letting it improve anyway. Even though my energy is low, to the point that I feel sluggish and ineffective, I am committed to doing whatever I can to improve.

Eyebrow	My energy is low
Side of the eye	This low energy
Under the eye	My very low energy
Under the nose	This sluggishness

Chin	Feeling physically tired
Collarbone	Feeling drained
Under the arm	My low, low energy
Top of the head	It feels like I'm running on empty
Eyebrow	My energy is low
Side of the eye	But I choose to feel light and free
Under the eye	This low energy
Under the nose	I choose to fill up with energy and potential
Chin	My very low energy
Collarbone	I now choose to feel light and free
Under the arm	My low, low energy
Top of the head	I am now filling up with energy and potential
Eyebrow	I choose to feel light and free
Side of the eye	I am filling with energy and potential
Under the eye	I choose to feel light and free
Under the nose	I am filling with energy and potential
Chin	I choose to feel light and free
Collarbone	I am filling with energy and potential
Under the arm	I choose to feel light and free
Top of the head	I feel energized, light, and free

I love to do tapping in which I alternate the negative statement with the positive statements. As I mentioned earlier, I find it most helpful to switch to positive affirmation statements after tapping on the negative statements for a while. For brevity, this example switched to positive much more quickly than I normally do when tapping on my issues at home.

Looking for Life's Sweetness

Hummingbirds certainly seem to be part of the sweetness of life. Every time I see one, I stop to watch. In fact, while I was writing this section, one flew by my window. The colors are so vibrant, and it makes me smile to watch how their little wings flutter so quickly. Hummingbirds also spend most of their time seeking out the sweetness in life, the nectar that is hidden in the flowers and feeders and seems to be nature's gift to them. So much of the time we spend focused on problems, trials, challenges, bitterness, and hostility when we could be focused on life's nectar—all of the things that happen that are blessings. We overlook them so readily. The next tapping is about the option to change our focus so that we are looking for the sweetness of life. Just imagine how pleasant that could be.

MPI: "I focus on the negative."

Setup (karate-chop point)—Even though I tend to focus on all of the problems in my life, I deeply and completely love and accept myself anyway. Even though I tend to focus on all of the problems in my life, to the exclusion of all of the great things I could be focusing on, I deeply and completely love, honor, and accept myself anyway. Even though I tend to focus on all of the problems in my life and miss out on so much happiness that way, I deeply and completely love and accept myself just as I am and choose to remain open to changing.

Eyebrow	Focus on the negative
Side of the eye	Focus on the negative
Under the eye	I focus too much on the negative
Under the nose	And seem to ignore the positive
Chin	This negative focus of mine
Collarbone	Too much negative
Under the arm	And not enough positive
Top of the head	I crave a change in focus
Eyebrow	There really are beautiful things everywhere
Side of the eye	If I only choose to see them
Under the eye	There is much sweetness in life
Under the nose	I just need to seek it out
Chin	And spend time enjoying it
Collarbone	I could revel in the sweetness of life
Under the arm	And feel so much better about myself and the world
Top of the head	That doesn't mean that I'm ignoring other important things
Eyebrow	Just that I would be in control of my focus
Side of the eye	The negative focus wouldn't be such a habit
Under the eye	Instead, the positive focus would be my habit
Under the nose	My default
Chin	And more difficult or negative things

Collarbone	Could claim my focus only when necessary
Under the arm	That would be wonderful
Top of the head	That would be delicious

This is another tapping exercise in which getting specific might intensify the experience in some pretty awesome ways. Try to add more sensory statements. When I did it, I included statements that described what some of the sweetness in life would be. I used visual imagery of flowers, hummingbirds, and butterflies. Other additions might include tasty things like apple pie, rich and creamy ice cream, and chocolate. Specific experiences or situations that represent the sweetness of life might include playing with a grandchild, witnessing the love at a wedding, or quiet times on the beach. Play with it and have fun.

Wrapping Up

In this chapter, we have considered several different characteristics associated with the hummingbird, including feeling unable to settle down, pessimism/optimism, cultivating a joyful heart, low energy, and actively seeking out the sweetness in life. A lot came up for me while I was tapping, including my difficulty finding balance between my generally optimistic attitude and my feeling that if I allow myself to express that optimism, I'm setting myself up for a huge letdown later. I found that pretty interesting, and I'm sure I'll have a lot of tapping to do on all of the experiences that have contributed to the imbalance.

An interesting thing about hummingbirds is that they can fly in any direction. They can go forward, backward, down, and up and can hover. How could you use that in your personal tapping? They also fly away and don't engage in discord or drama. I have some work to do on that one. Hummingbirds may also be asking if your heart is closed and whether you need to drop a judgmental attitude. Keep tapping with these qualities until you are ready to move to the next chapter about the owl.

14 Chapter

Owl

He respects Owl, because you can't help respecting anybody who
can spell TUESDAY, even if he doesn't spell it right.
—A. A. Milne

The first thing I think of when someone says "owl" is the Winnie the Pooh character. Descriptors from wise to pompous go through my mind, but I loved him all the same. I also think of X the Owl from *Mr. Rogers' Neighborhood*. I have three of his puppets, including King Friday XIII, X the Owl, and Lady Elaine, in my collection. I've often thought of getting rid of them but just can't seem to part with them.

Sitting on my desk watching over me while I write is a snowy owl (stuffed animal) that I purchased while in Sitka, Alaska. I was fortunate to visit the raptor center where they have many birds that are on display, being rehabilitated when possible, and awaiting release. All of the raptors were beautiful, but during the indoor presentation, the naturalist brought in a beautiful snowy owl. Although I'm sure she told us the owl's actual name, there was an audible whisper of "Hedwig" the minute the owl entered the room. Hedwig is the faithful companion of Harry Potter who carried messages and delivered mail for him.

As a totem, the owl may encourage cultivation of optimism, inspiration, and concentration while teaching us to avoid greed, gluttony, exaggeration, or overindulgence. Overall, the path of the owl is one that focuses on the need for balance and seeking opportunities to raise intellect and morality. Owl people conduct themselves proudly and are usually very inquisitive.

The Greek goddess Athena had a companion owl. Athena was known as the goddess of wisdom. The owl assisted her in speaking the whole truth instead of being limited by her blind side. Because of that association, the owl has been a symbol of knowledge, wisdom, and erudition.

I've never felt the owl to be a totem or spirit animal for me. That said, there are some owl encounters, mostly fictional, that created an emotional attachment. Reflect on your own owl experiences, and then please join me in the tapping meditation about owl characteristics.

Tapping Meditation

Eyebrow	Owl
Side of the eye	Bird of the night
Under the eye	Owl
Under the nose	All knowing
Chin	Owl
Collarbone	Able to see beyond illusion and deceit
Under the arm	Owl
Top of the head	Bearer of wisdom
Eyebrow	Owl
Side of the eye	Sign of life transition
Under the eye	Owl
Under the nose	The power of discernment
Chin	Owl
Collarbone	Able to uncover hidden potential and abilities
Under the arm	Owl
Top of the head	Truth
Eyebrow	Owl
Side of the eye	Patience
Under the eye	Owl
Under the nose	Darkness
Chin	Owl
Collarbone	Divination
Under the arm	Owl

Top of the head	Full of mystery
Eyebrow	Owl
Side of the eye	Protector of secrets
Under the eye	Owl
Under the nose	Messenger
Chin	Owl
Collarbone	What message do you have for me?
Under the arm	Owl
Top of the head	Open to the messages of the owl

Keep tapping while considering the knowledge experiences, and meaning that the owl has for you. Be sure to write down any thoughts, beliefs, or feelings that arise.

Feeling Uncertain

Think back to the last time you felt uncertain about something. For me, it was about two hours ago. It was a decision point, and I had already weighed the pros and cons but still had the queasy feeling in my gut. I decided that not making a decision was causing me more distress than making the decision.

Once you have a clear picture of your uncertainty situation, say the MPI, "I don't know how to do this."

Setup (karate-chop point)—Even though I don't know how to do this, I choose a path of wisdom. Even though I don't know how to do this, I choose a path of intellect. Even though I don't know how to do this, I choose the path of discernment.

Eyebrow	I don't know how to do this
Side of the eye	I don't know how to do this
Under the eye	I don't know how to do this
Under the nose	I don't know how to do this
Chin	I don't know how to do this
Collarbone	I don't know how to do this
Under the arm	I don't know how to do this

Top of the head	I don't know how to do this
Eyebrow	I don't know how to do this
Side of the eye	I choose to learn
Under the eye	I don't know how to do this
Under the nose	I choose to ask questions
Chin	I don't know how to do this
Collarbone	I choose to learn more about it
Under the arm	I don't know how to do this
Top of the head	I am developing the skills to be successful

For me, what comes next is being very specific about what it is I don't know how to do. I might also add tapping about how it feels to ask questions and what fear may be under that. I intend to tap about the moment of decision-making and how I want to feel while acting on my decision.

Intellectualizing

Once again, my thoughts return to Owl from Winnie the Pooh. That is the classic stereotype of intellectualization. Intellectualization has some benefit, including that it can keep us from taking action that we might be afraid to take. Instead, we can just sit and think about what action we might take. It also helps us to avoid the possibility of error. If we never take action, we don't have to face any negative consequences of taking an action, so therefore, we feel safe. The reality is that sometimes not taking action has real consequences too, so it might really be a false sense of safety.

MPI: "I would rather play the owl and intellectualize instead of taking action."

Setup (karate-chop point)—Even though I would rather play the owl and intellectualize instead of taking action, I deeply love and accept myself. Even though it feels like it would be more comfortable to think about the problems instead of taking action, I love, accept, and forgive myself. Even though I would prefer to think the problem away, I accept the reality of my situation and accept all of myself.

Eyebrow	I would rather play the owl
Side of the eye	Because then I can just think about it

Under the eye	Thinking is a good thing
Under the nose	If I really understand it, it could keep me from making a mistake
Chin	I'm very afraid of making mistakes
Collarbone	So, playing the owl keeps me safe
Under the arm	It also keeps me stuck
Top of the head	Intellectualizing isn't changing
Eyebrow	And I want my life to be different
Side of the eye	I want my life to be better
Under the eye	Thinking is good—but so is action
Under the nose	I already know what I need
Chin	I already know what I want
Collarbone	I know I can do it
Under the arm	Changing my life for the better is the wise thing to do
Top of the head	I know I can take action and succeed

People Don't Always Understand Me

Many people who have strong owl characteristics are found in the arts, and while they have adventurous spirits, they also frequently feel misunderstood by much of mainstream society. This may not seem an obvious characteristic for the owl, but it is good to remember that the owl is associated with many other things that are not understood and that people feel uncomfortable with owl characteristics and associations such as clairvoyance, the dark, sorcery, and witchcraft.

MPI: "I feel misunderstood."

Setup (karate-chop point)—Even though I often feel misunderstood, I choose to honor who I am and what I believe in. Even though I feel misunderstood, I deeply and completely love and accept myself. Even though I feel misunderstood, I love and accept my true nature.

Eyebrow	I feel misunderstood
Side of the eye	And somewhat detached from others
Under the eye	That isn't what I really want
Under the nose	Sometimes people see what they want to see
Chin	Not who I really am

Collarbone	Occasionally, that is a good thing
Under the arm	But usually it doesn't feel
Top of the head	The way I want things to feel
Eyebrow	I don't know how to get others
Side of the eye	To see the real me
Under the eye	I want to feel understood
Under the nose	I don't think that is such an unusual desire
Chin	I've worked hard to better understand myself
Collarbone	And now I want to let that shine through
Under the arm	I want others to better understand me
Top of the head	I choose to work toward that goal

Not Having the Answer Is Uncomfortable

Were you the child in the classroom who tried to be invisible so that you wouldn't be called on to answer a question in class? If it wasn't you, do you know someone who felt that way? Perhaps you took a different approach and overprepared so that there was very little risk of not knowing. I've been/done both. One of my favorite characters in the Harry Potter books is Hermione Granger because I can relate to her constant studying, almost immediate volunteering to answer any question, and her need to deal with the annoyance of others because of it. The next tapping addresses one aspect of that.

MPI: "I need to know all of the answers."

Setup (karate-chop point)—Even though not knowing the answer to something is uncomfortable for me, I choose to embrace the process. Even though not knowing raises my anxiety, I invoke the powerful message of the owl inside me and embrace the mystery as I discover the hidden answer. Even though not having the answer to everything has been uncomfortable for me in the past, I choose to honor and accept myself just as I am.

Eyebrow	I like to be the one with the answers
Side of the eye	It is pretty hard for me not to know
Under the eye	To me, not knowing means I am stupid
Under the nose	I heard that when I was growing up

Chin	And it was pretty scary
Collarbone	Bad things usually happened
Under the arm	When I was called stupid
Top of the head	It is no wonder that I don't like that feeling now
Eyebrow	I hate not knowing
Side of the eye	But I choose to embrace my owl wisdom
Under the eye	Sure, I may not know things
Under the nose	But I've developed the wisdom
Chin	To know how to learn or find answers
Collarbone	When my human uncertainty kicks in
Under the arm	I can connect with the spirit of the owl
Top of the head	I can feel powerful and wise

There are so many things to consider in this tapping in spite of its brevity. For one, it introduces the idea that wanting to be the one to answer questions or needing to know everything might have a different reason other than wanting to show off. Of course, there are people trying to show off, but even then, the reason for wanting to show off shouldn't be casually assumed. It also introduces the concept that there is a difference between knowing things and wisdom. If you could only have one, knowledge or wisdom, which would you choose? That could be another tapping exercise all by itself. Perhaps my favorite thing about this tapping example is the idea that all it takes to create change is to connect with the image of the totem animal. All of our associations with the owl in this case, or any other animal, are already there in our subconscious, so just thinking about the animal can help us access any of the characteristics we are currently lacking.

Not Feeling Smart

For some people, not feeling smart is a periodic occurrence, and for others, it is a well-developed self-concept. It is often just a bad habit to call ourselves "not smart" when we make a mistake. But if we repeat it over and over, we can actually come to believe it as a personality trait instead.

MPI: "I am not smart."

Setup (karate-chop point)—Even though I've never thought I was very smart, I love and accept myself. Even though I don't think I am very smart, I love and accept myself and acknowledge that I do have strengths. Even though I don't think I'm very smart, I choose to focus on my strengths and abilities.

Eyebrow	I am not very smart
Side of the eye	I am not very good at school
Under the eye	Some subjects were really hard for me
Under the nose	Things just didn't make sense sometimes
Chin	So, I must not be very smart
Collarbone	Other people picked things up very quickly
Under the arm	The teacher got impatient if I asked too many questions
Top of the head	I even heard kids talking about me
Eyebrow	They knew I wasn't smart
Side of the eye	I am not very smart
Under the eye	I didn't like school
Under the nose	I got bad grades
Chin	I'm not very smart
Collarbone	Not very smart
Under the arm	I don't do well with academics
Top of the head	It is hard for me to learn
Eyebrow	I always heard that I wasn't smart
Side of the eye	From just about everybody
Under the eye	And now I believe it
Under the nose	But what if they are wrong?
Chin	What is smart anyway?
Collarbone	I'm not very smart
Under the arm	But maybe I am
Top of the head	I'm great at solving puzzles
Eyebrow	Or taking things apart and putting them back together
Side of the eye	Isn't that smart too?
Under the eye	I'm not very smart
Under the nose	I'm good at understanding what my dog needs
Chin	And what my baby sister is saying
Collarbone	Even though no one else can understand her

Under the arm	Isn't that smart too?
Top of the head	Maybe, I'm smart at some things
Eyebrow	But not as smart at others
Side of the eye	Or maybe I'm already smart at some things
Under the eye	But not smart yet at others
Under the nose	I don't think anybody is really smart at everything at once
Chin	Maybe I just need some more time with some things
Collarbone	I choose to remember the things I am smart about
Under the arm	And continue to work on the things I'm not so smart about
Top of the head	I am okay

Wrapping Up

This chapter focused on only a few owl characteristics, including wanting to know how to do things, intellectualizing, wanting to be understood, feeling uncomfortable when answers are unknown, and not feeling very smart. What things did you notice when you were tapping? I had imagery pop into my mind about keen vision, both physically and intuitively. I also had some memories of engaging in lengthy discussions or arguments with the sole purpose of being right. That last one definitely suggests an owl characteristic that I might want to redirect in some way. I wrote several notes in my tapping journal for later. Take a look at what you wrote down. It might even be good to jot down a date for when you might tap about it.

The smallest owl is the elf owl, which is 5.6 inches tall and weighs 1.5 ounces. The largest owl is the North American great grey owl, which can be up to 32 inches tall. Do you need to do some tapping about size or comparisons you make with others? Owls cannot move their eyes and have to turn their heads in order to get a wide scope of vision. Perhaps we could need some tapping about things we see, can't see, or don't want to see. Barn owls mate for life, and they are actually known to cuddle with their mates and babies. Tapping about showing affection might be useful.

The next chapter is about the peacock. Most people usually immediately think of the beautiful tail feathers, but the peacock has so much more to offer.

15
Chapter

Peacock

I like peacocks and have always gotten excited when seeing them at the zoo. The first word that always pops into my mind is *exotic*. It was only recently that I found out that some people have them as pets. I had just never given them much thought. The only place I ever encountered them was at the zoo. A little research revealed that there are references to peacocks in many cultures throughout history, including folktales that suggest that peacocks were in the Garden of Eden, and they are mentioned in the Christian Bible as being part of the treasure of King Solomon.

In ancient Roman culture, peacocks represented funerals, death, and resurrection. It is said that they also became a symbol of immortality because their flesh, or at least their feathers, didn't decay after they died. In Greek mythology, the peacock was created from Argos Panoples, a hundred-eyed giant. When he died, Hera placed his eyes in the peacock's tail.

Beyond those characteristics just noted, the peacock is also associated with pride or arrogance because of the way it displays its spectacular tail and struts around. Spend a few minutes thinking about any peacock encounters you have had. Do they bring positive, neutral, or negative feelings when you think about them? As you begin the tapping meditation, open yourself to the message from the peacock.

Tapping Meditation

Eyebrow	Peacock
Side of the eye	Prideful
Under the eye	Peacock
Under the nose	Seeking recognition
Chin	Peacock
Collarbone	Arrogance
Under the arm	Peacock
Top of the head	Integrity
Eyebrow	Peacock
Side of the eye	Nobility
Under the eye	Peacock
Under the nose	Watchfulness
Chin	Peacock
Collarbone	Vibrant
Under the arm	Peacock
Top of the head	Glory
Eyebrow	Peacock
Side of the eye	Spirituality
Under the eye	Peacock
Under the nose	Refinement
Chin	Peacock
Collarbone	Appearances
Under the arm	Peacock
Top of the head	Benevolence
Eyebrow	Peacock
Side of the eye	Superficial
Under the eye	Peacock
Under the nose	Immortality
Chin	Peacock
Collarbone	What message do you have for me?
Under the arm	Peacock

Top of the head   Open to the message of the peacock

Keep tapping while considering the knowledge, experiences, and meaning that the peacock has for you. Be sure to write down any thoughts, beliefs, or feelings that arise.

Pride Is Getting in My Way

Does pride ever get in your way? Do you ever feel like a job is beneath you? Or maybe you think that your time is worth more than someone else's time. Are you completely sure that you know where this attitude comes from?

MPI: "Pride is getting in my way."

Setup (karate-chop point)—Even though pride seems to be getting in my way, I choose to work toward letting this go. Even though it seems like pride is standing in the way of reaching my goals, I choose to allow myself to move forward and grow. Even though pride is getting in the way again, I choose to love and respect myself.

Eyebrow	Pride
Side of the eye	Arrogance
Under the eye	Ego
Under the nose	Getting in my way
Chin	If I could just let it go
Collarbone	All of this pride
Under the arm	It doesn't make sense
Top of the head	Letting pride stand in the way of progress
Eyebrow	What is the purpose of this?
Side of the eye	How will this stubborn attachment help me?
Under the eye	Letting go of pride
Under the nose	Doesn't mean losing dignity
Chin	Letting go of pride
Collarbone	Doesn't decrease my value as a person
Under the arm	Letting go of arrogance and pride
Top of the head	I am open to the change

I Just Want to Blend In

There have been many times in my life when I did not want to stand out or be center stage. For example, one of my early ambitions was to be a backup singer. Granted, I do love creating harmony, but I believe that a large part was that I didn't want to be the center of attention. That felt vulnerable. It also felt like there was more responsibility and an increased risk for mocking and rejection.

MPI: "I don't like being the center of attention."

Setup (karate-chop point)—I'm uncomfortable being the center of attention. I deeply and completely love and accept myself. I just want to fade into the background. I love and accept all of me. It doesn't feel safe to stand out. I choose to allow myself the freedom to be me.

Eyebrow	I don't want to be the center of attention
Side of the eye	It makes me feel exposed
Under the eye	I worry about what others are thinking
Under the nose	I worry that they might be judging me
Chin	I like to be in the background
Collarbone	It feels safe there
Under the arm	But sometimes I do long for recognition
Top of the head	If only I could feel more self-assured
Eyebrow	If only I could be more confident
Side of the eye	I wouldn't really want to strut like a peacock
Under the eye	But I would like to be comfortable showing my true colors
Under the nose	I am open to learning more about this issue
Chin	And making a change if I want to
Collarbone	I choose to embrace who I am
Under the arm	In the spotlight or in the shadows
Top of the head	I choose to be me

I'm Too Shy

It might surprise you to see a tapping about being shy when we are in a chapter about the peacock. I don't think of the peacock as a shy animal. They roam freely all over the zoo, and while not overly friendly, they don't hide either. This is another example of looking at the other side of a characteristic. When the peacock spreads its beautiful tail or struts around, it is intending to be seen. For those people who identify themselves as shy, they often try hard not to be seen. Perhaps they need a little more peacock in their personality and can learn from this animal guide.

MPI: "I am shy."

Setup (karate-chop point)—Even though I am shy, I choose to love and accept myself just as I am. Even though I feel shy, I choose to love and accept myself just as I am. Even though people describe me as shy, I choose to love and accept myself just as I am.

Eyebrow	Feeling shy
Side of the eye	Feeling shy
Under the eye	Feeling shy
Under the nose	This shyness
Chin	I think I am shy
Collarbone	Other people have labeled me as shy
Under the arm	That must mean that I really am shy
Top of the head	People call me shy
Eyebrow	As if that is something that is wrong or bad
Side of the eye	They feel sorry for me because I'm not very outgoing
Under the eye	And seem to want me to feel bad because of it too
Under the nose	I wonder if anyone has ever been teased out of being shy
Chin	I sincerely doubt it
Collarbone	Being shy doesn't feel like a choice
Under the arm	It feels like it is who I am
Top of the head	But I wonder if that is really true
Eyebrow	I've been caught up in the belief that being shy is bad
Side of the eye	But I'm not sure that is really my own view
Under the eye	Sure, it isn't always comfortable
Under the nose	But that may be because of other people's response to my shyness
Chin	Rather than my own
Collarbone	I am open to understanding myself better

Under the arm	Even if others never understand me
Top of the head	Maybe shyness is a reaction
Eyebrow	Not a part of who I am
Side of the eye	If it is a reaction
Under the eye	I could change it when it feels right to me to change
Under the nose	And remain more reserved when my intuition leads me in that direction
Chin	Perhaps I have behaved more shyly in the past
Collarbone	Because it made sense at the time
Under the arm	I'm open to considering this on a case-by-case basis
Top of the head	I choose to love, honor, and believe in my ability to respond to situations intuitively and appropriately

If you have been labeled as shy, there are likely many specific instances that you can recall that would benefit from tapping. Consider tapping about the earliest incident you can remember in which someone called you shy. Focus on their tone of voice, facial expression, or another factor that led you to believe that being shy wasn't a good thing. You might also want to tap about a situation in which you felt you couldn't do or accomplish something because you were feeling shy and any regrets that may have resulted from that.

Arrogance

Has anyone ever called you arrogant? It can be a hard thing to hear, particularly if you feel that your behavior has been misunderstood. Imagine that, like the peacock, you have a feature, skill, or talent that is pretty spectacular. Are you supposed to pretend that you don't? When you are at the zoo, do you hope that the peacock will spread its tail, or do you scorn it when it does? I personally love to see that big, beautiful tail. There are times in our lives when we dare to shine, but other people call us arrogant or proud. I can remember several times when I felt proud of an accomplishment, and someone recited the "Pride goeth before a fall" admonition. That can make us worried and scared to express our greatness in any way. That is what the next tapping is about. It isn't really promoting arrogance. Instead, it is about discerning arrogance from appropriate pride in an accomplishment or situation.

MPI: "They think I am arrogant."

Setup (karate-chop point)—I hate being told that I am arrogant, particularly when I just feel like I'm being happy. It makes me reluctant to speak of the positive things that I've done, seen, or accomplished. Even with these jumbled-up feelings, I choose to deeply and completely love and accept myself. Even though I have a lot of unresolved feelings about being called arrogant and wanting to be happy about things I've done, I choose to remain calm and speak my truth. Even though being called arrogant could be a consequence of sharing my happiness with others, I choose to respect myself and anyone else who is involved in this situation.

Eyebrow	He called me arrogant
Side of the eye	And that really hurt
Under the eye	What also hurt
Under the nose	Is that I believed it
Chin	At the time, it seemed like he might be right
Collarbone	And maybe it wasn't okay to be happy about my success
Under the arm	But looking back
Top of the head	I'm pretty sure that I wasn't being mean
Eyebrow	I wasn't trying to make myself better than anyone else
Side of the eye	I wasn't gloating
Under the eye	I was just amazingly excited and happy
Under the nose	It is nice to receive awards
Chin	And it doesn't make sense to pretend that I don't enjoy it
Collarbone	I suspect he was just unhappy because he didn't get an award
Under the arm	And thought he could make himself feel better
Top of the head	By making me feel bad
Eyebrow	And I fell for it
Side of the eye	That may be the worst part of it for me now
Under the eye	I can be my own worst enemy
Under the nose	And it has stopped me from showing my happiness
Chin	Many times since that first incident
Collarbone	I have even tried to preempt the potential problem
Under the arm	By downplaying my successes before someone else can take me down
Top of the head	I don't get to feel happy then either
Eyebrow	I'm glad I care about how other people feel
Side of the eye	And I really don't want others to feel bad as a result of my successes

Under the eye	But for the most part, I can't control how they feel
Under the nose	I believe I should be careful
Chin	With my words, attitudes, and tone of voice
Collarbone	But if those remain appropriate
Under the arm	Someone else's reaction isn't because of me
Top of the head	They are completely responsible for their own response
Eyebrow	I choose to shine when I can
Side of the eye	Without flaunting or bragging
Under the eye	And know that expressions of pride and happiness
Under the nose	Can be completely appropriate
Chin	I affirm that happiness is *not* arrogance
Collarbone	I affirm that utilizing my strengths and assets
Under the arm	Is *not* arrogance
Top of the head	I affirm all that I am

Take a deep breath, and let it out. Notice if you are holding any tension in your body after completing this exercise. If you do notice tension, spend a few minutes tapping to release it from your body before moving on.

Appearance Is Only Skin Deep

Surely you've heard jokes about how long it takes women, and some men, to get ready to go somewhere. The classic examples include trying on multiple different outfits, spending hours on hair and makeup, and fretting about jewelry, handbag, and shoes. While I have at times been guilty of this, it is really quite rare for me. I know people who are habitually late for important events just because they are overly concerned about their appearance (not just poor time managers).

This type of behavior suggests an overemphasis on external appearance or perhaps a deep-seated belief or feeling that who they are on the inside is somehow inadequate or insufficient. While I can relate to those internal feelings, I've not been one to usually try to compensate with outward appearance, but it might be a familiar story for you. That is the topic of the next tapping, inspired by the beautiful outward appearance of the peacock.

MPI: "How I look determines who I am."

Setup (karate-chop point)—Even though I'm worried about how I look, because I think it says something important about who I really am, I deeply and completely love and accept myself anyway. Even though my appearance is pretty important to me, or at least I assume it is a pretty important factor in how others perceive me, I deeply and completely love and accept myself, and I choose to forgive myself, and anyone else, for contributing to this pattern or belief. Even though I am obsessively worried about my outward appearance, I choose to honor and accept myself, just as I am right now.

Eyebrow	How I look determines who I am
Side of the eye	How I look determines who I am
Under the eye	How I look determines who I am
Under the nose	How I look determines who I am
Chin	I'm afraid that how I look determines who I am
Collarbone	I am afraid that how I look is the most important part of who I am
Under the arm	I'm afraid that everything hinges on how I look and not who I am
Top of the head	That's silly
Eyebrow	No, it's not
Side of the eye	Yes, it is
Under the eye	No, it's not
Under the nose	People judge you on how you look
Chin	Well, at least some people do
Collarbone	And I care what *everyone* thinks about me
Under the arm	And I am unwilling to risk that they will think badly of me
Top of the head	If my hair, clothing, nails, shoes, and everything else isn't perfect
Eyebrow	That is crazy thinking
Side of the eye	No, it's not
Under the eye	Yes, it is
Under the nose	But it is *my* thinking
Chin	And I've been living my life that way
Collarbone	I know there isn't anything wrong with wanting to look nice
Under the arm	But maybe I do take it too far sometimes
Top of the head	It would feel better to not be so anxious about it

Eyebrow	This anxiety about how I look
Side of the eye	This appearance anxiety
Under the eye	This fear of judgment anxiety
Under the nose	This trying to control other people's opinions by being careful about how I look
Chin	This futile attempt to protect myself by trying to look perfect
Collarbone	It is exhausting
Under the arm	And futile
Top of the head	And I'm considering letting it go
Eyebrow	Or at least relaxing it a little bit
Side of the eye	Do I really want to care about whether my purse exactly matches my shoes?
Under the eye	No, I don't
Under the nose	Enough is enough
Chin	I choose to relax
Collarbone	It is time to believe that I am enough
Under the arm	With or without perfect jewelry
Top of the head	I am me, and that is enough

Keep tapping until you can say, "How I look determines who I am" with absolutely no feeling of truth.

Wrapping Up

It would be hard not to notice a peacock. They are simply stunning. In this chapter, we have considered a few characteristics associated with the peacock, such as pride, wanting to blend in, feeling shy, arrogance, and the concept that appearance is only skin deep. As noted at the beginning of the chapter, the peacock historically has been associated with funerals, death, resurrection, and immortality. I personally find it harder to relate to those issues when considering the peacock, but others may find some tapping guidance there.

Did you know that the peacock has eleven distinct calls? Perhaps you have tapping to do about finding your voice. One fact I found particularly interesting is that the female can lay "decoy" eggs some distance from the nest to confuse predators. This made me think about general tapping for safety, tapping for finding out-of-the-box (or nest) solutions to problems or possibly deceitfulness.

Peacocks don't get their colorful feathers until they are about three; then they lose them every year. This could prompt tapping about handling growth and development issues, maturity, or perhaps even the loss of physical beauty. I can assure you that some of these are already in my tapping journal for future work.

Our next totem animal is easily noticed when above ground, but much of their animal wisdom is hidden below. When I think about the prairie dog, I usually think of watching them pop up out of their tunnels or the times I've seen them wrestling around and seeming to have a great time.

16
Chapter

Prairie Dog

The first image I get in my mind when thinking about the prairie dog is of it standing up on its hind legs and looking around. I've always thought they were adorable, and in that pose, they look so inquisitive. Until I moved to New Mexico, I had only seen them in zoos. Now it is common to see them pretty much everywhere. One day, soon after arriving, I was waiting at a large intersection when two prairie dogs tumbled out of their burrow. They were wrestling with each other and nearly spilled into the street. I almost got rear-ended because I was busy watching them and not paying attention to traffic. I was captivated by their apparently carefree and playful behavior.

The prairie dog is a clan animal and known for its social structure. In some Native American cultures, the prairie dog is associated with the rain. There is a Jicarilla Apache myth that the prairie dog saved a warrior after the other forty-three members of his group had already died. The warrior was almost dead from dehydration when he collapsed near a prairie dog colony. The prairie dog is said to have invited the warrior into the den and gave him water, saving the man's life. Although I can't speak to the Apache interpretation of this event, it does fit with the prairie dog totem characteristic of community spirit.

Please join me in a tapping meditation to increase our connection to prairie dog wisdom.

Tapping Meditation

Eyebrow	Prairie dog
Side of the eye	Community
Under the eye	Prairie dog
Under the nose	Importance of touch
Chin	Prairie dog
Collarbone	Affection
Under the arm	Prairie dog
Top of the head	What lies beneath the surface?
Eyebrow	Prairie dog
Side of the eye	Philanthropy
Under the eye	Prairie dog
Under the nose	Social skills
Chin	Prairie dog
Collarbone	Renewed success
Under the arm	Prairie dog
Top of the head	Expressed feelings
Eyebrow	Prairie dog
Side of the eye	Seeking rewards
Under the eye	Prairie dog
Under the nose	Inner peace
Chin	Prairie dog
Collarbone	Prosperity
Under the arm	Prairie dog
Top of the head	Ready to retreat
Eyebrow	Prairie dog
Side of the eye	Stillness of mind
Under the eye	Prairie dog
Under the nose	Playfulness
Chin	Prairie dog
Collarbone	What messages do you have for me?
Under the arm	Prairie dog

Top of the head	Open to the message of the prairie dog

Keep tapping while considering the knowledge, experiences, and meaning that the prairie dog has for you. Be sure to write down any thoughts, beliefs, or experiences that arise.

Looking beneath the Surface

Prairie dogs are pretty cute. I know that some people don't like them because they can carry rodent diseases and can be destructive, but they are just so much fun to watch. In addition to that, their system of hills and tunnels is downright amazing. When you look at a prairie dog habitat, the majority of it is beneath the surface.

There are probably many ways to look at this from a totem or spirit animal viewpoint. What popped up for me first was how often I get stuck thinking, feeling, or reacting to what is most obvious rather than stopping to look for the deeper or hidden meaning. I can recall numerous times when that has led me to make decisions that were either ill-informed or only somewhat effective. At this particular time in my life, that is probably my personal growth message from the prairie dog. Other potential messages might include making sure that there is a strong foundation or adequate underpinning for your decisions or actions, always allowing for an escape route, or making sure that there are pops of fun and sunshine in your otherwise low-level day. You will need to decide what message the prairie dog has for you based on your own life circumstance. In the meantime, tap along with the next exercise.

MPI: "I make snap decisions."

Setup (karate-chop point)—Even though I tend to make snap decisions without having all of the information to make a good one, I deeply and completely love and accept myself. Even though I tend to take things at face value without really thinking about what is contributing to what I see, I deeply and completely love and accept myself anyway. Even though I tend to see what is on the surface, I love, honor, and accept myself.

Eyebrow	Making snap decisions
Side of the eye	Making decisions too quickly
Under the eye	Making decisions without all of the information
Under the nose	Taking things only at face value

Chin	Ignoring what might be below the surface
Collarbone	Not looking or understanding deeply enough
Under the arm	Sometimes works out okay
Top of the head	Because my intuition is pretty good
Eyebrow	But sometimes it doesn't work out
Side of the eye	And I'm sure I could do better
Under the eye	If I understood why something is the way that it is
Under the nose	May not make it any better
Chin	And it might not make it any worse
Collarbone	It will allow me to act on the real problem
Under the arm	Instead of just responding to what is on the surface
Top of the head	Looking for what is underneath
Eyebrow	Discerning the below-the-surface view
Side of the eye	Incorporating a total view
Under the eye	Into my response patterns
Under the nose	Rather than taking things only at face value
Chin	This more total approach
Collarbone	Feels a lot more like wisdom
Under the arm	And I like that
Top of the head	This is definitely an area where I can grow

As I have mentioned before, you may want to write down some specific experiences that you have had in which you made snap decisions that did not go so well for you. Also, if you have a good idea of how you would like to respond differently and can include that in your tapping, I predict some amazing results.

I'm an Introvert

It is true. I am an introvert. That doesn't mean that I don't like people. That would be antisocial—against people. The reality is that there are so many things I like to do that don't require any other people, and I can entertain myself for days, weeks, or months with only limited social contact. That is in stark contrast to the prairie dog. Prairie dogs are highly social creatures. They live in large family units and twenty or more of these family units can band together to form a prairie dog town. There isn't a lot of personal space in these prairie dog towns, so they really have to be social in order to make that work well. Honestly, I'm glad I'm not a prairie dog. There could be a message for me though. I sometimes feel that I might be missing out on something because I'm not more social.

MPI: "I am an introvert."

Setup (karate-chop point)—Even though I am an introvert and not everybody is okay with that, I deeply and completely love and accept myself. Even though I am an introvert and not everybody is okay with that, I choose to honor my own tendencies and preferences, as long as I am sure that they are still working for me and are what I really want. Even though I am an introvert and sometimes it feels like I am living in a world of extroverts where I don't really fit in, I choose to love, honor, and accept myself, and consider ways that I could be more social when it really suits me.

Eyebrow	I am an introvert
Side of the eye	And really okay with it
Under the eye	At least most of the time
Under the nose	I don't want to act like an extrovert
Chin	For me, it would be exhausting
Collarbone	Too much stimulation
Under the arm	Too much drama
Top of the head	I really do prefer the quieter life of introversion
Eyebrow	At least most of the time
Side of the eye	But what about the time when
Under the eye	I'm not okay with it
Under the nose	What about when I notice that the extroverts are having fun that I'm not having
Chin	I could join in
Collarbone	They are extroverts. They are going to want more people to come out and play
Under the arm	I bet it is as hard for them to be alone and still
Top of the head	As it is for me to be the life of the party
Eyebrow	Choosing to accept my way of being
Side of the eye	Not because it is better
Under the eye	Not because it is worse

Under the nose	Just because it is my way of being
Chin	I'm open to seeing my introversion through another person's perspective
Collarbone	And I could even ask them to include me sometimes
Under the arm	In some of their activities
Top of the head	I would like to be a little more flexible about this
Eyebrow	To not be so in the habit of being by myself
Side of the eye	That I miss out on the fun tidbits of life
Under the eye	I really do want to be part of a community
Under the nose	But I want my own level of connectedness
Chin	To be on my own terms
Collarbone	I know I need alone time
Under the arm	But I'm finding I need some social time too
Top of the head	Adapting to my growing desire for some social connection

One of the things addressed in the tapping was the need to be adaptable. In that case, it was adapting the needs of an introvert to the benefits of some more social activities. We can all get trapped in ways of living or responding that worked for us at one time of life but as we grow and mature may not be serving our needs any longer.

Seeing the Options

Prairie dogs want options. If you look at their tunnels, there is never just one way out. There are always contingencies, and they appear to be well considered. Being able to see options, whether it is an escape route, alternate solution to a challenge, or methods for creating love and happiness can be a great benefit for all of us.

MPI: "Times are tough right now."

Setup (karate-chop point)—Even though times are tough right now, I choose to feel relaxed and calm. Even though things I'm facing are challenging, I choose to remain relaxed and calm. Even though it looks like things might get worse before they get better, I choose to remain relaxed and calm.

| Eyebrow | Things are tough |

Side of the eye	It is a tough time
Under the eye	This time of challenge
Under the nose	This time of uncertainty
Chin	Feeling uncomfortable
Collarbone	Pushing ahead
Under the arm	But do I have to?
Top of the head	Is there another way?
Eyebrow	Or can I build in some alternatives?
Side of the eye	I don't have to keep moving forward
Under the eye	If forward doesn't make sense anymore
Under the nose	That isn't giving up
Chin	It is having a strategy
Collarbone	Or a contingency plan
Under the arm	And knowing how to use it
Top of the head	Having room to maneuver
Eyebrow	To make it work
Side of the eye	I need to be relaxed and calm
Under the eye	To see my options
Under the nose	And then decide what I want to do
Chin	Exercising my choices
Collarbone	While feeling relaxed and calm
Under the arm	Using my contingencies
Top of the head	While feeling relaxed and calm

Laying the Groundwork

What do you imagine goes into the complex network of dens and tunnels that comprises a prairie dog community, whether in captivity or in the wild? I doubt that they just start digging and whatever happens is just random. Whether by instinct or intellect, the prairie dog knows what it needs and endeavors to create a solid foundation for its survival.

MPI: "I have a tendency to just jump right in."

Setup (karate-chop point)—Even though I like immediate action and immediate results, I deeply and completely love and accept myself. Even though I would prefer to just dive in and go for the goal instead of spending time planning and preparing, I deeply and completely love and accept myself. Even though I would like to just charge forward and get the job done, I deeply and completely love and accept myself.

Eyebrow	Getting it done
Side of the eye	Crossing it off my list
Under the eye	Moving on to something else
Under the nose	Those are things I prefer
Chin	And that strategy often works well for me
Collarbone	But sometimes it doesn't
Under the arm	Like the prairie dog, sometimes it would be best to delay
Top of the head	And lay the groundwork
Eyebrow	Establish a foundation
Side of the eye	Before charging forward
Under the eye	That can be hard for me
Under the nose	Not the planning. I'm a good planner
Chin	Not the part where I anticipate problems or failures
Collarbone	I'm really good at that too
Under the arm	I'm not sure what the problem is
Top of the head	But I'm sure that I have room to grow
Eyebrow	Jumping in
Side of the eye	Total commitment
Under the eye	Versus waiting
Under the nose	Thinking it through
Chin	Digging and laying a foundation
Collarbone	I can do this when it is appropriate
Under the arm	Or I can implement immediately if need be
Top of the head	Adjusting to the demands of the situation
Eyebrow	Choosing to remain flexible
Side of the eye	Open to more clarity
Under the eye	Appreciating the groundwork
Under the nose	And appreciating action too

Chin	Getting it done is important
Collarbone	Getting it done right is important too
Under the arm	The groundwork is part of the success plan
Top of the head	And I choose to be more attentive to this part

During this tapping, I kept hearing the phrase, "Go big, or stay at home." As I continued to tap with that phrase, I became aware that I sometimes interpret that saying to mean that I shouldn't play it safe. I also became aware that playing it safe doesn't always mean playing small. Such as the case with the prairie dog, laying the groundwork or playing it safe is just an acknowledgment that we must attend to safety and one way to do that is with prior planning.

Playfulness

What words do you associate with play? Perhaps you associate play with childhood or childishness. Other people associate play with wasting time or failure to accomplish tasks. For children and adults, play can enhance creativity, exercise imagination, develop dexterity, and improve physical, cognitive, and emotional functioning. We can also consider play from a different angle. Play, or playfulness, can be an attitude that is present even when doing work. It includes the choice to have fun or not take things so seriously. While there are tasks that I cannot see as play, such as scrubbing toilets or doing dishes, perhaps a more playful or less serious attitude would decrease my avoidance.

MPI: "I'm not having fun."

Setup (karate-chop point)—Even though I'm not having nearly as much fun as I'd like to have, I choose to increase my capacity for fun every day. Even though my life seems more like work than it does play, I choose to schedule some time for play every day. Even though I'm feeling uncomfortable about committing to more fun and play in my life, I choose to remain open to the possibility that I'm really going to love it.

Eyebrow	Not having fun
Side of the eye	I think I've forgotten how to play
Under the eye	Everything feels so serious
Under the nose	So important
Chin	And only children play anyway

Collarbone	So why would I want to commit to playing more
Under the arm	Do I want people to call me childish?
Top of the head	No, of course not
Eyebrow	I want to be seen as a competent adult
Side of the eye	Even though I don't think being an adult is all that great
Under the eye	This contrast
Under the nose	Wanting more fun and play
Chin	But also wanting achievement and success
Collarbone	I seem to act like they are mutually exclusive
Under the arm	But are they?
Top of the head	I know some people talk about working hard and playing hard
Eyebrow	But that hits me as working hard
Side of the eye	And then working hard again on things that are supposed to be fun
Under the eye	If I weren't working so hard at them
Under the nose	Considering having more fun
Chin	Considering what kind of play I might enjoy
Collarbone	I'm pretty sure I can be a grownup and still play
Under the arm	Exploring the options
Top of the head	Considering more play

Wrapping Up

While prairie dogs are not likely my personal totem, I really do like them, and I found them an interesting animal to tap about. In this chapter, we tapped about looking beneath the surface, making snap decisions, introversion/extroversion, seeing multiple options, and laying the groundwork for success. I made a note in my tapping journal to tap about some other prairie dog characteristics in the future, including finding a sense of community, my feelings about physical touch, and philanthropy. Make a note of any prairie dog characteristics you would like to see more or less of in your life.

Another way to use totem animals is to consider what their predators are. Prairie Dog predators include coyotes, hawks, eagles, and badgers. If you feel that any of these might be your totem animal, tapping about the prairie dog might be beneficial.

I learned a few new facts about the prairie dog that might guide some future tapping. The prairie dog colonies also provide shelter for other animals, including jack rabbits, toads, burrowing owls, and rattlesnakes. I found this pretty interesting since I would think that a prairie dog would be incompatible with a rattlesnake. Take a few minutes to consider what this might teach us about sharing our environment and resources. The entire mating season for the prairie dog only lasts for one hour. In spite of this, their populations in many places are continuing to expand. My first thought is that this could spark some tapping about making the most of small windows of time or looking for the best possible outcomes in a situation. And finally, they live in family groups called coteries. These family groups are essential to their survival. Perhaps we could grow in the way that we interact with our own family group.

Our next totem animal feels very different to me than the prairie dog, perhaps because I have a strong aversion to scorpions. While it was tempting to exclude it from the book, I felt it was important to include creatures that I don't like. Take a few minutes to think about your feelings and experiences with the scorpion before moving on to the next chapter.

17

Scorpion

When I moved to New Mexico, I knew that I would be seeing many new mammals, insects, and birds. Admittedly, there were several that I was keen to see and others that I had no desire to encounter. One of those creatures I have a strong aversion to is the scorpion, and I knew they were common in New Mexico. I had seen them in movies, photos, and glass aquariums. I think I actually prefer the dead specimens in the science museum.

I had been in New Mexico several months, dutifully scanning the ground when I was out walking to be sure that neither I nor my dogs stepped on one. One morning, while walking barefoot in my house, I opened the pantry door to grab an item from the shelf when I spotted something on the floor right where I would have stepped next. There was a baby scorpion in my pantry. It was only about an inch long, but I screamed. I panicked. I was afraid to kill it and thought about trapping it and releasing it outside, but I never want to encounter a scorpion outside either, so what was I supposed to do?

The legend of the horse and scorpion stuck in my mind. That scorpion, had I not tried to kill it, wasn't going to remember me later and spare me from injury should we run into each other again. It was going to do what scorpions do—*sting*. I'm not particularly proud of myself, but I tried to kill it with bug spray. I thought I had it too. I put so much bug spray on it that I was pretty sure that it drowned. Much to my surprise, when I went back (with thick gloves on) to scoop it into the trash can, it was gone.

Why was the scorpion there? It might have been hunting. It might have gotten lost. It might have been there to offer me a lesson. On that day, the lesson that seemed to hang in the air was one of being careful. This carefulness could include my need to be careful with what I say and how I say it so that my words don't sting others or with where I go or even the need to wear shoes.

In ancient Egyptian mythology, the scorpion was associated with the goddess Serqet. She is usually depicted with a scorpion on her head and associated with spells used to avoid and cure venomous bites. The god Shed was also linked to protection against scorpion stings. The scorpion was sacred to Isis, and another scorpion goddess was Tabitjet.

What lesson might a scorpion bring to you? To answer that question, let's do a tapping meditation to get in touch with some of the characteristics associated with the scorpion and to get ready for whatever messages the scorpion might have for you.

Tapping Meditation

Eyebrow	Scorpion
Side of the eye	Retaliation
Under the eye	Scorpion
Under the nose	Destruction
Chin	Scorpion
Collarbone	Pain
Under the arm	Scorpion
Top of the head	Mystical
Eyebrow	Scorpion
Side of the eye	Change
Under the eye	Scorpion
Under the nose	Defensiveness
Chin	Scorpion
Collarbone	Biting truth

Under the arm	Scorpion
Top of the head	Control
Eyebrow	Scorpion
Side of the eye	Transition
Under the eye	Scorpion
Under the nose	Death and dying
Chin	Scorpion
Collarbone	Passion
Under the arm	Scorpion
Top of the head	Treachery
Eyebrow	Scorpion
Side of the eye	Solitary
Under the eye	Scorpion
Under the nose	Secretive
Chin	Scorpion
Collarbone	What message do you have for me?
Under the arm	Scorpion
Top of the head	Open to the message of the scorpion

Keep tapping while considering the knowledge, experiences, and meaning that the scorpion has for you.

Feeling the Pain

Pain is no fun. Not only is there the intensity of the physical sensation, but there is also the weariness from prolonged pain and the emotional distress that results from whatever caused the pain, the fact that you have the pain, and any concerns you have that it might never go away. The scorpion reminds us of pain. Just look at that stinger. Ouch!

Tapping is a great tool for managing pain. Unfortunately, when I am in pain, I am in a primitive response mode and need someone else to remind me to tap since I don't seem to have access to all of my coping responses when pain is really bad. It was very useful in managing pain during physical therapy after knee surgery. At first, I tapped about my emotional response to experiencing pain, including how out of control I felt. That brought me back into what I call *adult rational mode*, and then I was able to tap to reduce the pain itself. Nick Ortner of the Tapping Solution has a great book dedicated to using tapping for pain relief that you may want to read if pain is an issue for you. The next lesson is about coping with pain. Rate your current level of distress about your pain.

Setup (karate-chop point)—Even though I am in a lot of pain right now, I choose to relax and let my body heal naturally. Even though I am in a lot of pain right now, I choose to relax and allow healing to take place. Even though I am in a lot of pain right now and I'm not sure how much longer I can stand it, I choose to love myself and allow my body to relax and heal.

Eyebrow	This pain
Side of the eye	This pain in my …
Under the eye	This pain
Under the nose	I hate having this pain
Chin	It hurts
Collarbone	It upsets me
Under the arm	I don't want it
Top of the head	I want it to stop
Eyebrow	It is not fair that I have it
Side of the eye	It makes me angry
Under the eye	And feeling angry
Under the nose	Makes the pain worse
Chin	Fighting against my body
Collarbone	Makes the pain worse
Under the arm	I have this pain in my …
Top of the head	It feels like a …
Eyebrow	If it had a color, it would be …
Side of the eye	If it had a shape, it would be …
Under the eye	If it had a sound, it would be …
Under the nose	Feeling the pain
Chin	And trying not to react to it
Collarbone	It is just information
Under the arm	And I can choose how to respond
Top of the head	This pain in my …

Eyebrow	I choose to relax
Side of the eye	This pain in my ...
Under the eye	I choose to allow healing
Under the nose	This pain in my ...
Chin	I choose to seek health
Collarbone	I remain calm and relaxed
Under the arm	I choose to respond appropriately
Top of the head	I choose to allow healing in my body

To get the most out of the tapping, remember to personalize these exercises. If you tapped with the words as written, go back and tap again using your specific pain. Be sure to add the descriptors about location, pain sensation, shape, color, and so on. Some clients have complained that it feels silly to assign a color or shape to their pain, but when they do it, they generally experience the benefit. Anything that helps to focus attention on the pain deepens the tapping experience and increases the likelihood of relief. When talking about pain, relief is what it is all about.

Sharp Words

Lots of things can sting. Some that come to mind are mosquitos, bees, ants, jellyfish, antiseptics, and of course scorpions. The physical ones we can avoid most of the time, but words can sting too. They make us feel bad and seem to hang around, continually irritating us for quite a while, just like an insect sting.

MPI: "My sharp words hurt others."

Setup (karate-chop point)—Even though I often say things without thinking them through and hurt other people with my sharp words or tone of voice, I choose to love, honor, and forgive myself. Even though I often say things without thinking them through and hurt other people with my sharp words or tone of voice, I choose to love, honor, and forgive myself. Even though I often say things without thinking them through and hurt other people with my sharp words or tone of voice, I choose to love, honor, and forgive myself.

Eyebrow	My sharp words
Side of the eye	Hurting others

Under the eye	Don't intend to
Under the nose	But it happens anyway
Chin	I can tell by the expression
Collarbone	That my words stung a little
Under the arm	Or sometimes a lot
Top of the head	And I feel bad afterward
Eyebrow	But then it is too late
Side of the eye	My sharp words
Under the eye	Often need to be softer
Under the nose	More caring
Chin	More compassionate
Collarbone	More thoughtful
Under the arm	Reducing my sharp words
Top of the head	My sharp words

Continue tapping about specific instances in which someone used words that hurt you and those times when your words hurt someone else. I would recommend adding tapping about how you would like to handle the situations in the future too.

Revenge

To be fair, I don't think the scorpion is really out for revenge. Scorpions are just doing what scorpions do. But if I'm really honest, it feels like revenge. It is hard to imagine someone or something hurting me unless a general hatefulness or desire for revenge is involved. Although I am loath to admit it, I frequently experience a desire for revenge when someone has hurt me. Fortunately, it is briefer than in the past, but my primitive response of wanting to hurt them back still exists. It generally isn't a desire to physically hurt someone, but I do want them to feel the same or more emotional pain than I'm feeling.

MPI: "I want revenge."

Setup (karate-chop point)—Even though I really want to strike back and hurt him as much as he just hurt me, I choose to love, accept, and care for myself and to honor these strong feelings. Even though I want to get revenge because of the pain I'm feeling right now, I acknowledge how much I'm hurting, and I choose to focus on taking care of myself first. Even though I'm appalled by how strongly I want revenge for all of this pain he inflicted on me, I choose to remain calm, remove myself from any danger, and then reassess my responses.

Eyebrow	Wanting revenge
Side of the eye	Wanting revenge
Under the eye	Wanting revenge
Under the nose	Wanting revenge
Chin	Wanting revenge
Collarbone	Wanting revenge
Under the arm	I don't like this feeling
Top of the head	Wanting revenge
Eyebrow	I don't know what to do
Side of the eye	Wanting revenge
Under the eye	This feeling is very strong
Under the nose	Wanting revenge
Chin	I acknowledge that this is a normal and expected feeling
Collarbone	Very primitive and very real
Under the arm	I can choose to respond to it
Top of the head	In many different ways
Eyebrow	Or not at all
Side of the eye	My feelings are just feelings
Under the eye	They are important
Under the nose	But they do not control me
Chin	This is just my body's way
Collarbone	Of trying to keep me safe
Under the arm	Trying to make sure he doesn't hurt me again
Top of the head	I'm thankful that my body
Eyebrow	Is trying to take good care of me
Side of the eye	But I also know
Under the eye	Revenge isn't the only option I have
Under the nose	Not wanting to be hurt
Chin	But I know revenge isn't my best answer

Collarbone	Getting revenge
Under the arm	Won't make me feel better for long
Top of the head	I need to handle this in a better way

I'm Alone

Does anyone really want to be with a scorpion? Maybe the ancient Egyptians, but I certainly don't. I don't necessarily believe that the scorpion has any feelings about being alone, but most people do. Either you welcome alone time, or you avoid alone time at all costs. Generally speaking, the reason that you are alone also impacts how you feel about it. If you are choosing it because you want to get something done, I expect that you don't associate that episode of being alone with anything negative. I love it when I get some alone time like that. There have also been times, and I'm sure you can relate, when being alone feels like rejection. That is the situation considered in the next tapping.

MPI: "I feel rejected."

Setup (karate-chop point)—Even though I'm feeling rejected and alone right now and it feels like no one wants to be with me, I choose to feel peaceful and content. Even though I'm feeling alone and I'm afraid no one wants to spend time with me, I choose to feel peaceful and calm. Even though I'm feeling rejected and like no one will ever want to spend time with me, I choose to get involved in something that can raise my spirits, even a little bit, right now.

Eyebrow	Feeling rejected
Side of the eye	No one wants to be with me
Under the eye	No one likes me
Under the nose	It will always be this way
Chin	I've been rejected
Collarbone	I'm alone
Under the arm	And it is probably all my fault
Top of the head	I choose to feel peaceful instead of upset
Eyebrow	I choose to feel content instead of upset
Side of the eye	I choose to relax
Under the eye	I choose to be calm

Under the nose	I choose to move on
Chin	Instead of dwelling on this negative feeling
Collarbone	I will look at this later
Under the arm	When I am ready to learn from it
Top of the head	Or to implement a change
Eyebrow	But for right now
Side of the eye	I'm feeling rejected
Under the eye	And instead, I choose peace
Under the nose	Right now, I feel nobody wants to be with me
Chin	Instead, I choose to focus on feeling content
Collarbone	With who I am
Under the arm	And what I have
Top of the head	Right now, it feels like no one likes me
Eyebrow	In the face of this
Side of the eye	I choose to relax
Under the eye	Right now, it feels like it will always be this way
Under the nose	And I choose to move on
Chin	Right now, I'm feeling alone
Collarbone	Instead, I choose to focus on the people who do like me
Under the arm	Right now, I'm feeling rejected
Top of the head	But I choose to focus on times when I've felt included instead

Keeping Secrets

Most people just don't understand scorpions. They have been around forever, and they can do things that are hard to understand. It is as if they are keeping secrets. In the story of the horse and the scorpion, the scorpion tricks the horse into carrying it over water into safety. What it didn't tell the horse was that it was going to sting it anyway. That is a pretty big secret.

MPI: "I'm keeping secrets."

Setup (karate-chop point)—Even though I have this secret I'm keeping, I deeply and completely love and accept myself. Even though I'm keeping secrets and I'm unsure about whether that is a good thing or not, I deeply and completely love and accept myself. Even though I keep a lot of secrets, I am making the choice to deeply and completely love and accept myself.

Eyebrow	Keeping secrets
Side of the eye	Keeps me safe
Under the eye	Keeping secrets
Under the nose	Keeps me safe
Chin	Keeping secrets
Collarbone	Keeps me safe
Under the arm	Afraid of what would happen
Top of the head	If anyone knew my secrets
Eyebrow	Keeping secrets
Side of the eye	Keeps me safe
Under the eye	Afraid of what people would think
Under the nose	If they knew my secrets
Chin	Keeping secrets
Collarbone	Keeps me safe
Under the arm	Keeping secrets
Top of the head	Keeps me safe

Wrapping Up

In this chapter, we have tapped about pain, sharp words, getting revenge, rejection, and keeping secrets. Messages from the scorpion can also be about destruction, defensiveness, and treachery. Remember that although these seem pretty dark and most people will want to reduce these factors in their own personalities, tapping on the opposite or nearly opposite characteristic can be just as useful. You can think of it as tapping in the counterbalance to those negative qualities.

Scorpions are not passive insects; they are considered predatory arachnids and are carnivores. Although more common in the desert, they are present on every continent except Antarctica. Shocking to me, in addition to insects and spiders, they can also eat lizards and small rodents. Perhaps this might be a good image when you are facing a David and Goliath situation in which you feel like David. Scorpions do have one "talent" that I would very much like to have. They can slow their metabolism down so much that when food is unavailable, they can live off of just one insect for an entire year. They also speed up their metabolism when food is abundant. That is the part I want.

You can't talk about scorpions without talking about survival mentality. Scorpions are estimated to have been around for more than 400 million years. They know how to survive for the long haul. Tapping about adaptation, survival, and staying relevant in a changing world might be some options that would be beneficial.

Our next chapter is about another animal who has mastered the art of survival. Turn the page and dive into some tapping about the shark.

18 Chapter

Shark

I wish you could hear me. I'm humming the song from the movie *Jaws*. That is one of the first things I think about when considering the shark. I have also had some personal experiences with a variety of different types of shark while scuba diving in the Galapagos Islands. I'll admit to being a very reluctant diver in shark-filled waters. I didn't mind so much when we were seeking hammerhead sharks or whale sharks. In spite of their size, they are pretty safe. One day, while I was scuba diving, one of the men in my group tried to signal me to join him. He was literally in the middle of a circle of fifteen to twenty sharks. Okay, it was possibly only ten, but there was no way I was going to go out there. It was fun to watch from a distance though.

When I was younger, I did a lot of water skiing. This was usually in local rivers and lakes. I once had the opportunity to water ski in salt water, possibly the Gulf of Mexico but more likely on the east coast of Florida. I do remember that it was pretty fun, but toward the end, the people in the boat were getting frustrated because I wouldn't quit. Not long after starting, I remembered something that my father had said to me about the possibility of sharks in that water, and I was too afraid to stop. Eventually, they had to cut the motor in order to get me to quit.

I have also enjoyed time at the Newport Aquarium, standing in the glass tunnels and watching sharks swimming on all sides of me. I admit that I still startle when one comes right up beside me. Have you ever put your hand in one of those children's hands-on exhibits to touch a shark? I've done it but was pretty nervous even though the shark was less than a foot long.

If you dare to enter the water, join me in a tapping mediation about the shark.

Tapping Meditation

Eyebrow	Shark
Side of the eye	Hunter
Under the eye	Shark
Under the nose	Survival
Chin	Shark
Collarbone	Adaptability
Under the arm	Shark
Top of the head	Self-trust
Eyebrow	Shark
Side of the eye	Calculating
Under the eye	Shark
Under the nose	Perceptive
Chin	Shark
Collarbone	Instinctive
Under the arm	Shark
Top of the head	Ancient
Eyebrow	Shark
Side of the eye	Lethal
Under the eye	Shark
Under the nose	Powerful
Chin	Shark
Collarbone	Dynamic
Under the arm	Shark
Top of the head	Superior
Eyebrow	Shark
Side of the eye	Effective

Under the eye	Shark
Under the nose	Perpetual motion
Chin	Shark
Collarbone	What message do you have for me?
Under the arm	Shark
Top of the head	Open to the message of the shark

Keep tapping while considering the knowledge, experiences, and meaning that the shark has for you. Be sure to write down any thoughts, beliefs, or feelings that arise.

Keep Moving Forward

Most but not all sharks have to keep swimming all of the time to pull water into their gills in order to breathe. Can you imagine always needing to be in motion? Perhaps the opposite is sometimes problematic in your life. Instead of moving, you feel stuck and unable to move forward. Or perhaps worse, maybe it feels like you are going backward.

MPI: "I'm stuck."

Setup (karate-chop point)—Even though I feel like I'm really stuck right now, I choose to love and accept myself anyway. Even though I feel like I'm really stuck right now, I choose to relax and allow myself to make whatever changes I need to make so that I can move forward. Even though I feel like I'm really stuck right now, I accept myself and all of the factors and circumstances that have led me to this point.

Eyebrow	I'm stuck
Side of the eye	Feeling stuck
Under the eye	Want to move forward
Under the nose	But for some reason, I can't
Chin	I'm just stuck
Collarbone	And it seems like I can't get unstuck
Under the arm	Feeling stuck
Top of the head	I've been stuck for a while
Eyebrow	And the more I fight against it

Side of the eye	The more stuck I feel
Under the eye	Maybe I could just relax
Under the nose	And allow the next step forward
Chin	To show up in my life
Collarbone	I can visualize myself moving forward
Under the arm	And get a sense of what that would feel like
Top of the head	I can allow the things that are keeping me stuck
Eyebrow	To fall away effortlessly
Side of the eye	So that I can move forward
Under the eye	Easily and effectively
Under the nose	Without struggle
Chin	Without fighting
Collarbone	I'm stuck now
Under the arm	But I won't stay that way
Top of the head	I'll move forward again

Adaptation

Much like the scorpion, the shark has been around a long time. Estimates are that sharks have inhabited the waters for 455 million years. Although it is believed that they look almost exactly the same based on fossil records, you know that they have had to adapt in some ways to the changing condition of our oceans over that many years.

One thing is certain, we all have to change. The world is continually changing, and so are the daily demands. Some people seem to be able to adapt to those changes more easily than others. In evolutionary terms, the organisms that can adapt are able to survive or even thrive. The organisms that can't or won't adapt to change don't survive. Which would you prefer? Unfortunately, I'm not one of those folks who adapt easily. I like my comfort zone. I like my routine. Change often causes me anxiety.

MPI: "I hate change."

Setup (karate-chop point)—Even though I hate change, I choose to relax and adapt. Even though I hate change, I choose to love myself, including my disdain for change. Even though I hate change, I choose to remain open to seeing this differently in the future.

Eyebrow	I hate change
Side of the eye	I hate change
Under the eye	I hate change
Under the nose	I hate change
Chin	I hate change
Collarbone	I hate change
Under the arm	I hate change
Top of the head	I hate change
Eyebrow	I hate change
Side of the eye	But I choose to adapt
Under the eye	I hate change
Under the nose	But it is better than extinction
Chin	I hate change
Collarbone	But I can learn to do it more easily
Under the arm	I hate change
Top of the head	But I am open to seeing the possibilities
Eyebrow	I choose to allow change to happen more easily
Side of the eye	So that I can adapt to a changing world
Under the eye	I choose not to be obsolete
Under the nose	I choose not to be extinct
Chin	And that requires change
Collarbone	Learning to adapt more easily
Under the arm	Mastering this skill
Top of the head	Letting go of my limiting beliefs about change

Thick Skin

Sharks have very interesting skin. First, their skin can be up to six inches thick. But even more appropriate to this tapping is that their skin has little scales, called dermal denticles, that help reduce the friction when they swim. When considering the admonition to get a thicker skin so that we aren't feeling so vulnerable, like the shark, we are just trying to reduce the friction from the words other people hurl at us.

MPI: "I need a thicker skin."

Setup (karate-chop point)—Even though I felt upset when they told me I needed to grow a thick skin, I choose to love and accept myself anyway. Even though I harbor resentment about when he told me I needed to get a thicker skin, I choose to love and accept myself totally and completely, thick skin or not. Even though I apparently don't have a thick enough skin for some people's liking, I love, honor, and accept who I am.

Eyebrow	I am so angry
Side of the eye	I don't need a tougher skin
Under the eye	I need people to be decent human beings
Under the nose	Blaming me for a thin skin
Chin	Is just him not taking responsibility
Collarbone	For being mean
Under the arm	It is so unfair
Top of the head	I hate being blamed
Eyebrow	For his bad behavior
Side of the eye	Sure, if I had a "thick skin"
Under the eye	He wouldn't have to self-monitor
Under the nose	He could say whatever he wanted
Chin	And I would just take it
Collarbone	But this event is over now
Under the arm	And it is still bothering me
Top of the head	A lot
Eyebrow	It certainly isn't hurting him
Side of the eye	But it is hurting me
Under the eye	Because a part of me
Under the nose	That part that couldn't fight back
Chin	Believed it
Collarbone	I believed that I was the problem
Under the arm	That I needed a thick skin
Top of the head	But now I know better, and I choose to relax and let it go

Instincts

I find it hard at times to rely on my instincts. For much of my life, people in charge have made me question whether my instincts were valid and reliable. It happened in some subtle and not-so-subtle ways. For example, were you ever so angry as a child that you told a grown-up that you hated someone, and they responded by telling you that you didn't really hate the person? Maybe you had an experience in which you felt frightened, but you were told that what you were afraid of wasn't really scary. I've had both done to me and have done it to others. Being told that what I was feeling was wrong made me less able to trust my own primal powers and instincts. Although I'm doing better, I find it hard to rely on my gut, even though it is pretty accurate.

MPI: "I'm afraid to trust myself."

Setup (karate-chop point)—Even though I find it hard to listen to my gut, I deeply and completely love and accept myself. Even though I often second guess myself when it comes to following my instincts, I am learning to love that part of myself again.

Eyebrow	Afraid to trust my gut
Side of the eye	Afraid to trust myself
Under the eye	Afraid to trust my inner guidance
Under the nose	Afraid to trust my primal nature
Chin	Afraid to follow my intuition
Collarbone	Trained to believe they are right and I am wrong
Under the arm	Even about my own feelings
Top of the head	And my own experiences
Eyebrow	When I have trusted my gut
Side of the eye	It has been amazingly spot on
Under the eye	But much of the time
Under the nose	I don't even listen for it anymore
Chin	Or worse, I ignore it
Collarbone	Bad things usually follow
Under the arm	When I ignore an instinct or gut feeling
Top of the head	Learning to trust again
Eyebrow	Learning to trust myself again
Side of the eye	Not giving up on the facts

Under the eye	But acknowledging a knowing that is sometimes beyond the facts
Under the nose	Knowing what I feel
Chin	My feelings can't be wrong
Collarbone	It doesn't mean that I have to react to them
Under the arm	All of the time
Top of the head	But I can learn to hear my inner voice again and reclaim my primal power

Survival

How would you define survival mode? For me, it is the sense of treading water, not really moving forward in my life, but trying hard not to slip backward. This might occur in response to some recent stressor that drains all of my current resources, or it might be about larger concepts of survival of the species over millions of years like the shark. Trying to help the species exist for millions of years seems very overwhelming for me, so the next tapping is about just trying to stay alive, either literally or figuratively.

MPI: "I'm in survival mode."

Setup (karate-chop point)—Even though I'm in survival mode right now, I deeply and completely love and accept myself. Even though I'm in survival mode right now, I choose to react with peacefulness and hope for the future. Even though I seem to be in survival mode right now, I choose to feel relaxed and calm.

Eyebrow	Survival mode
Side of the eye	Going through the motions
Under the eye	Just to stay alive
Under the nose	No fun
Chin	No joy
Collarbone	Just trying to make it to tomorrow
Under the arm	Trying to survive
Top of the head	Survival
Eyebrow	Necessary
Side of the eye	Survival mode
Under the eye	Wanting something more

Under the nose	Fighting for survival
Chin	Taking it one day at a time
Collarbone	Trying to survive
Under the arm	Just keep going
Top of the head	Trying to survive

Wrapping Up

We have spent time in the shark-infested waters, tapping about feeling stuck or the need to keep moving, the necessity of adaptation, having a thicker skin, and survival mode. Some of the things I noticed when tapping with shark characteristics was how very strong my survival instinct is. I was considering the many times in my life when I was in some way bullied, threatened, or victimized and how rare it was for me to just passively "accept my fate." Instead, I am much more likely to fight back if there is any chance at all that it will increase my survival odds. However, I also noticed that I may need to develop more empathy with others who do not respond to these types of challenges the way I do and instead take a more passive stance. Spend a few extra minutes and consider anything that you noticed about the way you express or reject the shark characteristics before moving on.

As usual, I wanted to share some additional shark fun facts with you that might spark some additional tapping ideas. The shark can only swim forward. Can you imagine living life where you could only go forward? I can see both positive and negative ways that this could impact our lives. It might keep us from backing away from a challenge, but perhaps it could compel us forward into a really dangerous situation. It really bothers me, but the shark has the largest brain of any fish. I would prefer to think of them as nothing but brawn with no brain. I plan to do some tapping for clarity about that. I'm not sure why I would have a preference at all. Sharks are the only fish to have eyelids. This made me think of tapping about things I do and don't want to see. Because I feel the need to leave you with a more "negative" image of sharks, they eat their siblings and can be carnivorous in the womb. This definitely makes me think of tapping about sibling rivalry.

We climb back on dry land in the next chapter to follow the sheep as it guides us to the concepts of innocence, vulnerability, and following social norms. That should be quite the contrast to shark energy.

19
Chapter

Sheep

Sheep are pretty common in rural Ohio. They were just around. I wasn't aware that I had any strong feelings about sheep at all until one day I was visiting a friend's house and there was a lamb outside in her yard. I don't remember why it was there, I don't remember why it wasn't there the next time I visited, but I do remember soon after that, I was given an opportunity to eat lamb (not at her house) and couldn't possibly consider eating it. Fast-forward to adult years, and I was still refusing to eat lamb, so at Easter, my mother-in-law tried to trick me into eating it by telling me it was roast beef. I knew that roast beef wasn't usually served with mint jelly so didn't fall for the trick.

Sheep reentered my awareness again many years into my psychology practice. I had a client who was very much into working with fibers and spinning her own yarns. She taught me a lot about different types of sheep, fleece, and fiber.

Sheep have been prominent in many different religions and mythologies. For example, in Egypt, the god Khnum had the head of a ram. In Madagascar, sheep were considered human reincarnations and were not eaten. In the Chinese zodiac, sheep/rams are prominent and represent sensitivity, creativity, insecurity, and anxiety. Lambs and shepherds are prominent figures in the Christian Bible.

Consider your experiences with and feelings about sheep, whether from personal encounters, religion, or literature, and join me in the opening tapping meditation.

Tapping Meditation

Eyebrow	Sheep
Side of the eye	Innocence
Under the eye	Sheep
Under the nose	Vulnerability
Chin	Sheep
Collarbone	Childlike
Under the arm	Sheep
Top of the head	Conformity
Eyebrow	Sheep
Side of the eye	Social norms
Under the eye	Sheep
Under the nose	Self-acceptance
Chin	Sheep
Collarbone	Weakness
Under the arm	Sheep
Top of the head	Powerlessness
Eyebrow	Sheep
Side of the eye	Desire for belonging
Under the eye	Sheep
Under the nose	Need for self-care
Chin	Sheep
Collarbone	Respecting own limits
Under the arm	Sheep
Top of the head	Lost
Eyebrow	Sheep
Side of the eye	Scattered
Under the eye	Sheep
Under the nose	Needing guidance

Chin	Sheep
Collarbone	What message do you have for me?
Under the arm	Sheep
Top of the head	Open to the message of the sheep

Keep tapping while considering the knowledge, experiences, and meaning that the sheep has for you. Be sure to write down any thoughts, beliefs, or feelings that arise.

Taking Direction

Sheep are known as followers. People often describe sheep as being unable to think for themselves and willing to follow the herd off the edge of a cliff because they are just following the sheep in front of them. I have never personally witnessed this, but I certainly get the idea. Some people are natural leaders, and some are more naturally followers, but we are all generally called on at some point to fulfill the role that is opposite for us. The difficulty in doing that is strong for both types of people. In this tapping, we are going to look at the difficulty of a natural leader trying to assume a follower role.

MPI: "I'm not good at taking direction."

Setup (karate-chop point)—Even though I'm sometimes not so good at taking direction from others, I deeply and completely love and accept myself. Even though I tend to like to do things my way and therefore sometimes have trouble taking direction from others when they are in charge, I deeply and completely love and accept myself. Even though I sometimes have difficulty taking direction from others, I deeply and completely love and accept myself.

Eyebrow	I did it again
Side of the eye	I should have just said, "Yes, sir!"
Under the eye	But instead, I had to ask a bunch of questions
Under the nose	I don't think I even really wanted the answers
Chin	I was just showing off
Collarbone	How much I already knew about this
Under the arm	Then, I didn't completely follow the directions
Top of the head	I had to make it better

Eyebrow	At least better in my mind
Side of the eye	There's nothing wrong with wanting to improve things
Under the eye	But sometimes that is not my role
Under the nose	And I have trouble accepting that
Chin	Again, sometimes I'm just showing off
Collarbone	And trying to make myself look good
Under the arm	That's not always bad either
Top of the head	I wish I were better at taking direction
Eyebrow	It is a skill that needs development
Side of the eye	That way, I wouldn't upset others
Under the eye	Quite so much
Under the nose	I'd like to let go
Chin	Of always needing it my way
Collarbone	Choosing to take direction
Under the arm	When I'm not the one in charge
Top of the head	Choosing to take direction more easily

Indecision

Sheep are frequently characterized as indecisive and, as a result, not likely to survive when a quick life-saving decision is needed. You wouldn't want someone with the personality characteristics of sheep to be the one to have your back in a disaster. However, a sheep might be great if you want someone to follow you with blind faith. As a totem or spirit animal, perhaps the sheep is suggesting you need to work on making quick decisions, stop any second-guessing, or learn to commit to a course of action. Conversely, this totem could suggest that you are overly abundant in those qualities to your detriment and instead need to learn to consider your decisions more carefully. Remember, the lessons from a totem can go both ways.

MPI: "I can't make a decision."

Setup (karate-chop point)—Even though I can't seem to make a decision right now, I love and accept myself anyway. Even though making decisions seems almost painful to me, and I'm so stuck on getting it right that I can't even do it, I love and accept myself. Even though I keep second-guessing any decision I try to make, I love and accept myself.

Eyebrow	Can't make a decision
Side of the eye	Can't make a decision
Under the eye	Can't make a decision
Under the nose	Can't make a decision
Chin	Can't make a decision
Collarbone	Can't make a decision
Under the arm	Can't make a decision
Top of the head	Can't make a decision
Eyebrow	Can't make a decision quickly
Side of the eye	Can't make a decision
Under the eye	Can't make a decision confidently
Under the nose	Can't make a decision
Chin	Second-guessing my decisions
Collarbone	Can't make a decision
Under the arm	It is hard for me to make a decision
Top of the head	Can't make a decision
Eyebrow	I am open to clarity
Side of the eye	Can't make a decision
Under the eye	But I choose to believe that even this can improve
Under the nose	Can't make a decision
Chin	I choose to relax
Collarbone	Can't make a decision
Under the arm	I choose to love myself
Top of the head	Can't make a decision
Eyebrow	I choose to honor myself
Side of the eye	Can't make a decision
Under the eye	I choose to respect myself
Under the nose	Can't make a decision as easily as I would like
Chin	At least I haven't been able to in the past
Collarbone	Difficulty making a decision
Under the arm	Until now
Top of the head	I choose to love, honor, and accept myself

I recommend using this tapping or something similar whenever you feel stuck.

Old Mistakes—New Beginnings

Sheep, in particular lambs, are a sign of rebirth or new beginnings. They can be the herald for giant do-overs or subtle changes that take us gradually on a new path. These new beginnings can be exciting or terrifying. How do you feel about altering course or starting over? Honestly, I'm not a fan.

MPI: "I'm afraid to try something new."

Setup (karate-chop point)—Even though I have a new opportunity, I'm tempted to hang on to the job I've got. I may not like it, but it is less scary than pursuing something new. Even though I'm feeling this inner conflict, I choose to remain relaxed and calm. Even though I have the possibility of a new job, I've also got this sick feeling in my gut that is holding me back. In spite of this feeling, I choose to remain relaxed and calm. Even though I'm afraid of the prospect of a new beginning, I choose to remain relaxed and calm.

Eyebrow	Afraid to try something new
Side of the eye	To start over
Under the eye	To begin again
Under the nose	To make a change
Chin	I say I want it
Collarbone	I'm ready for it
Under the arm	But my body is saying something different
Top of the head	It is in my gut
Eyebrow	This sick feeling in my gut
Side of the eye	This sick feeling in my gut
Under the eye	This sick feeling in my gut
Under the nose	This sick feeling in my gut
Chin	It is trying to keep me safe
Collarbone	But instead it is keeping me stuck
Under the arm	Afraid to start over
Top of the head	Afraid to begin again

Eyebrow	I wonder what it is that I'm really afraid of?
Side of the eye	How do I know that making a change isn't safe?
Under the eye	How do I know that not making the change keeps me safe?
Under the nose	The truth is that I don't know
Chin	I believe in relying on my intuition
Collarbone	But sometimes I need to be rational about it too
Under the arm	If I choose not to make a change
Top of the head	That is okay
Eyebrow	If I choose to make a change
Side of the eye	Or to start over
Under the eye	That is okay too
Under the nose	But I choose not to be ruled by fear
Chin	Caution is okay
Collarbone	But fear is not
Under the arm	I love and accept myself, even with this reluctance to change
Top of the head	I love and accept myself just as I am right now

Black Sheep

Sheep are all about conformity. I bet when you think about sheep, the mental image is of an animal that is white. What about the black ones? In our society, the term *black sheep* has a negative connotation, but I've always really liked the black ones. Perhaps that is a statement about what I think of conformity in general or how poorly suited I am for conformity. If the sheep resonates with you or keeps showing up in your life, perhaps there is a lesson awaiting you about conformity.

MPI: "I am the black sheep."

Setup (karate-chop point)—Even though I feel like the black sheep of the family and I simply don't fit in, I deeply and completely love and accept myself. Even though I feel like the black sheep of the family, I deeply and completely love and accept myself. Even though I don't fit in and feel like the black sheep, I deeply and completely love and accept myself.

Eyebrow	I am the black sheep

Side of the eye	I just don't fit in
Under the eye	And it is pretty noticeable
Under the nose	Not just to me
Chin	But to them too
Collarbone	I wouldn't mind so much
Under the arm	But the comments can really hurt
Top of the head	I don't understand
Eyebrow	Why it is a problem for them
Side of the eye	It is not usually a problem for me
Under the eye	I like black sheep
Under the nose	I like their uniqueness
Chin	I love it that they are different
Collarbone	I don't really want to be like everybody else
Under the arm	But I also don't want to be treated badly
Top of the head	Just because I am different
Eyebrow	Black sheep doesn't mean I'm bad
Side of the eye	Or that I've done something wrong
Under the eye	It just means
Under the nose	I'm making my own way
Chin	Charting my own course
Collarbone	And I don't want to apologize for that
Under the arm	I am the black sheep
Top of the head	And I choose to allow myself to feel pretty good about that

Conformity

The previous tapping inspired by the black sheep was somewhat about conformity but specific to the feeling of not fitting in. In the next tapping, we are going to address the concept of conformity more directly. It was written specifically about conformity regarding food issues because of my food allergies and the discomfort and pressure I feel when eating with other people, but it can be applied to most other issues as well.

There is a time in most of our lives when conformity is the primary goal. For me and many others, this time is middle school. There is such a herd mentality. The worst thing you can imagine is being viewed as different from the rest. Different includes such trivial things as wanting to buy lunch at school instead of bringing it from home if that is what everyone else is doing, even if you don't like the food. Some people continue this path of conformity and would run right off the proverbial cliff to be like everyone else, and other people develop their own codes of living. Tapping about specific instances in which your conformity or lack thereof had some sort of lasting impact could be quite enlightening and a great opportunity for growth.

MPI: "I feel different."

Setup (karate-chop point)—Even though I hate feeling different and to me that often means feeling less than, I choose to love, honor, and respect myself and to forgive myself and anyone else who has contributed to this feeling. Even though it feels awkward to be different, like when I'm eating different food than everybody else, I choose to love, honor, and respect myself for putting my own needs as a high priority. Even though I really dislike all the looks and questions about my behaviors that are different, I choose to love, honor, and respect my current decision that such conformity would not benefit me in the long run.

Eyebrow	Conformity
Side of the eye	Conformity
Under the eye	Others wanting me to conform
Under the nose	Knowing it could seem easier
Chin	And desperately wanting to be accepted
Collarbone	By my family, my friends, my tribe
Under the arm	Conformity has its place I'm sure
Top of the head	But not always
Eyebrow	And I have all of these messed-up feelings about it
Side of the eye	Like when people comment about the food I eat
Under the eye	Or try to get me to take just a little taste
Under the nose	Of something that will surely make me sick or uncomfortable
Chin	I'm proud of my ability to stick to my healthy diet
Collarbone	But I also feel the pressure to conform
Under the arm	I know this was an example of early programming
Top of the head	But I don't really remember when it started for sure

Eyebrow	I want to be able to separate belonging
Side of the eye	From conformity
Under the eye	I am open to understanding more about this
Under the nose	And letting go of any fear that I have
Chin	That failure to conform may mean rejection
Collarbone	I am also open to understanding more
Under the arm	About how to handle these situations
Top of the head	With grace and dignity

Wrapping Up

The sheep offered opportunities to tap about taking directions, indecision, seizing new opportunities, feeling like we don't fit in, and conformity. Be sure to write down any thoughts or experiences you had while tapping about these characteristics. You may also want to do tapping on some of the other totem characteristics of the sheep that were mentioned in the opening tapping meditation, such as innocence, social norms, and feeling lost.

The Navajo churro is the oldest breed of sheep in the United States. That might inspire tapping about being an elder. Just that word brings up a lot of emotion. Each sheep produces about eight pounds of fleece in a year. That speaks to me of patience, the gradual accumulation of desired accomplishments, or the shedding of excess, like in the fleecing process. A baby sheep is about the same size as a human baby, five to eight pounds. This could spark tapping about the pain of childbirth or the irresistible cuteness of infants (sheep and human) that makes you just want to lapse into baby talk.

We are going to get down in the dirt for the next chapter and tap about the characteristics of the snake. Many people have a strong aversion to snakes, and it might be tempting to just skip the chapter. If you choose to skip it, I hope that you will come back to it later. Much can be learned from tapping about animals that we don't like or have a bit of a phobia about.

20
Chapter

Snake

I don't particularly like snakes. I wouldn't say I'm phobic, but I prefer them far away or in zoo enclosures. I've done some tapping about my dislike of snakes and have managed to decrease my anxiety significantly as long as they don't surprise me. While tapping, I became aware that part of my aversion is that they eat animals I really like, and I think the way they go about eating is pretty icky too. I have a very strong memory of a snake in my high school, probably biology class, eating a live mouse. Not a fan!

Snakes are represented in the mythology of many different cultures. In the African cultures, an ancient dog created the sun, moon, earth, and twins that were half human and half snake. In Central America, the ancient Mayans claimed that the first people to inhabit the Yucatan were people of the snake. In Egypt, the snake was associated with immortality and often depicted on tombs carrying the pharaoh to the land of the gods. The snake was particularly associated with the four primeval goddesses of water, invisibility, infinity, and darkness. Apep was a water snake and demon of the underworld.

The Celts associated the snake with wisdom, fertility, and immortality, and there are many references to the serpent in the Christian Bible associated with evil or Satan. In Native American cultures, the snake is associated with fertility and rebirth.

More recent snake associations for me come from the short story "Riki Tiki Tavi" by Rudyard Kipling, Kaa from *The Jungle Book*, and the basilisk and Lord Voldemort's snake, Nagini, who are both prominent in J. K. Rowling's Harry Potter books. If you dare, join me in the tapping meditation about some of the totem characteristics of the snake.

Tapping Meditation

Eyebrow	Snake
Side of the eye	Primal energy
Under the eye	Snake
Under the nose	Healing
Chin	Snake
Collarbone	Transformation
Under the arm	Snake
Top of the head	Spiritual guidance
Eyebrow	Snake
Side of the eye	Shrewd
Under the eye	Snake
Under the nose	Fertility
Chin	Snake
Collarbone	Rebirth
Under the arm	Snake
Top of the head	Observant
Eyebrow	Snake
Side of the eye	Surprise
Under the eye	Snake
Under the nose	Intuition
Chin	Snake
Collarbone	Supernatural power
Under the arm	Snake
Top of the head	Acceptance
Eyebrow	Snake
Side of the eye	Unconscious drives

Under the eye	Snake
Under the nose	Slow to anger
Chin	Snake
Collarbone	What message do you have for me?
Under the arm	Snake
Top of the head	Open to the message of the snake

Keep tapping while considering the knowledge, experience, and meaning that the snake has for you.

Transformation

The transformational power of the snake totem is exemplified by the shedding of the snake's skin. It is a physical rebirth process. Additionally, it teaches us that we can transform most things that come into our lives, for better or worse. We can create opportunity out of loss, passion from hardship, or vitality from illness. Consider the ways in which you have engaged in the process of transformation. Are there things in your life or personality that you would like to transform now?

MPI: "I'm facing this hardship."

Setup (karate-chop point)—Even though I am facing this hardship right now, I choose to remain open to learning how to use this experience to create a better opportunity. Even though I am facing this hardship right now, I choose to remain open to using this experience for growth and prosperity. Even though I am facing this hardship right now, I choose to remain hopeful and full of expectation for the great things that are coming next.

Eyebrow	This hardship
Side of the eye	Things are really hard right now
Under the eye	And I'm having trouble seeing past this moment
Under the nose	All I can focus on
Chin	Is this hardship
Collarbone	And how bad it feels
Under the arm	This hardship

Top of the head	Stuck in this negative viewpoint
Eyebrow	I'm having a hard time
Side of the eye	But I choose to remember that things can transform
Under the eye	Into something wonderful
Under the nose	This hardship
Chin	And I choose to remember that things can transform
Collarbone	Into something special
Under the arm	This hardship
Top of the head	I can transform it
Eyebrow	Seeking transformation
Side of the eye	Things will change
Under the eye	Transforming hardship into something wonderful
Under the nose	Things do change
Chin	Transforming hardship into something special
Collarbone	Transforming hardship into something better
Under the arm	Things change
Top of the head	I claim this transformational power

Staying Grounded

While snake energy can represent ambition, creation, and dreaming, the physical presence of the snake on the ground teaches us that it is important to remain grounded in reality. Both the lofty spiritual aspects and remaining grounded in our environment are desirable. Many people get lost in one realm or the other. I've known many creative dreamers who fail to take care of daily life activities. I've also known people who are so wrapped up in the mundane aspects of daily living that they forego their opportunities to create or to dream. Are you aware of your tendencies? Spend some time reflecting on your own need for snake wisdom, and then say the starting statement, "I have no time or energy to be creative."

Setup (karate-chop point)—Even though I feel like I don't have time to consider my hopes and dreams because I'm so busy trying to survive, I choose to take a deep breath and relax, allowing myself the freedom to be myself. Even though I feel like I don't have time to even have a dream or to be creative, I choose to love, honor, and accept myself and all of the chaos that is my life. Even though I feel like I have to spend every waking and sleeping moment getting things done or being ready for the next crisis, I deeply and completely love and accept myself and look forward to a time when I can express my creativity more fully.

Eyebrow	I used to have my head in the clouds
Side of the eye	Daydreaming
Under the eye	Making things up
Under the nose	Coming up with plans for my future
Chin	Visualizing
Collarbone	Allowing my mind to roam freely
Under the arm	Full of aspirations
Top of the head	Until life got in the way
Eyebrow	Actually, I was criticized for dreaming
Side of the eye	And they told me to be more practical
Under the eye	People made fun of my hopes and dreams
Under the nose	And I was told I couldn't achieve them
Chin	For one reason or another
Collarbone	Including the fact that I am a girl
Under the arm	Somehow, that was an immediate limit
Top of the head	So, I buckled down and got busy
Eyebrow	I'm good at that too
Side of the eye	I can accomplish a lot
Under the eye	And eventually I forgot to dream
Under the nose	I tell myself that I got too busy
Chin	And that if I stopped juggling my life tasks for even a minute
Collarbone	It would all come crashing down
Under the arm	But I'm not sure that is totally the truth
Top of the head	Being busy became my habit
Eyebrow	Being busy actually protected me from criticism
Side of the eye	And embarrassment
Under the eye	And that worked for a while
Under the nose	But it isn't working so well now
Chin	I want some of that creativity back
Collarbone	But what if it's gone?

Under the arm	What if I missed my chance?
Top of the head	Is it too late?
Eyebrow	The snake tells us
Side of the eye	It is never too late to transform
Under the eye	In fact, transformation is an ongoing process
Under the nose	It is happening, even when we are unaware
Chin	So, it is never too late
Collarbone	I can be more creative
Under the arm	I can allow myself to dream
Top of the head	While still managing my life's tasks
Eyebrow	It doesn't have to be all or nothing
Side of the eye	But it could be sometimes one or sometimes the other
Under the eye	Or it could be both at the same time
Under the nose	I get to choose
Chin	If it feels scary, I can back off if I want to
Collarbone	Or go full steam ahead
Under the arm	There isn't a right answer
Top of the head	The freedom to remember my ability to dream and create

Fertility

The snake, as a totem or spirit animal, is associated with sexuality, the life cycle, and fertility—yes, fertility in terms of procreation but also fertility as it relates to the ability to create or produce crops, money, or opportunities. Perhaps you are having difficulty creating a new human life. Perhaps your fields, literally or figuratively, are not as fertile as what you would like. The appearance of the snake as a totem animal may be telling you that you need to work on the energetic, physical, or emotional blocks that are limiting your creative power. Having fertility issues of any variety will also come with a load of emotional baggage, such as regret, frustration, sadness, confusion, self-loathing, blame, or fear. Each of these reactions to fertility issues should probably be the topic for some tapping as well. I hope you are feeling comfortable doing that kind of specific tapping on your own after all of this practice. In the meantime, tap along with this more general exercise about fertility.

MPI: "Yearning for more fertility."

Setup (karate-chop point)—Even though my level of fertility isn't what I want it to be right now, I choose to love and accept myself. Even though my level of fertility isn't what I want it to be right now, I choose to view myself as whole and complete. Even though my level of fertility isn't what I want it to be right now, I choose to relax and treat myself with love and compassion.

Eyebrow	Not fertile
Side of the eye	Not fertile
Under the eye	Not fertile
Under the nose	Not fertile
Chin	Not fertile
Collarbone	Not fertile
Under the arm	Not fertile
Top of the head	And it sucks
Eyebrow	I feel incomplete
Side of the eye	I feel "less than"
Under the eye	I feel frustrated
Under the nose	I feel betrayed
Chin	I feel blocked
Collarbone	I feel angry
Under the arm	I feel incompetent
Top of the head	And it sucks
Eyebrow	I am worthy of love
Side of the eye	I am worthy of respect
Under the eye	I am worthy of peace
Under the nose	I am worthy of joy
Chin	My fertility isn't a sign of my worthiness
Collarbone	My fertility isn't a sign of my humanity
Under the arm	My fertility isn't a sign of my usefulness
Top of the head	It is just a state of being
Eyebrow	My fertility might change
Side of the eye	My fertility might not change
Under the eye	But that doesn't change who I am
Under the nose	I feel incomplete
Chin	It sucks

Collarbone	But I am worthy of love
Under the arm	I feel less than
Top of the head	It sucks
Eyebrow	But I am worthy of respect
Side of the eye	I feel frustrated
Under the eye	It sucks
Under the nose	But I am worthy of peace
Chin	I feel betrayed
Collarbone	It sucks
Under the arm	But I am worthy of joy
Top of the head	My fertility
Eyebrow	I feel blocked
Side of the eye	It sucks
Under the eye	But my worthiness isn't in question here
Under the nose	I feel angry
Chin	It sucks
Collarbone	But my humanity is intact
Under the arm	I feel incompetent
Top of the head	It sucks
Eyebrow	I am quite useful
Side of the eye	I am worthy of love
Under the eye	I am worthy of respect
Under the nose	I am worthy of joy
Chin	I am worthy of peace
Collarbone	I am worthy
Under the arm	With or without increased fertility
Top of the head	I am worthy

Change Is Painful

You might find this ironic, I know I do, but I really don't like change. My first practice actually was called Choices Changes Attitudes, and I felt compelled to help other people positively embrace the concept of change. I believed then, and still do, that change is essential to our growth and happiness. That belief doesn't really change my experience of pain when change is necessary or forced upon me though. I'm still working on it.

Say that aloud: "Change is painful." It seems like a reasonable statement to me. While snake energy is generally considered to be symbolic of change, if we look at it from the contrary view, it can also be a sign of our fear of change. Many people cling to the "devil I know is better than the one I don't know" philosophy or harbor the belief that change is painful. These are limiting beliefs, and tapping is very effective in reducing or eliminating them. It is true that sometimes we experience discomfort when leaving the safety of our current rut; however, it is not true that all change is painful. Do you notice this negative self-fulfilling prophecy in your life? If so, you may have this or some other limiting belief about change that keeps you from moving forward with desirable changes.

MPI: "Change is painful."

Setup (karate-chop point)—Even though I believe that change is painful, I deeply and completely love and accept myself and this limiting belief. Even though I believe that change is always painful, I deeply and completely love and accept myself in spite of this limiting belief. Even though I believe that change is always painful, I deeply and completely love and accept myself even with all of my limiting beliefs.

Eyebrow	Change is painful
Side of the eye	Change is always painful
Under the eye	Everybody knows this
Under the nose	It is an irrefutable truth
Chin	Or is it?
Collarbone	Of course it is
Under the arm	Change is always painful
Top of the head	That is not true
Eyebrow	Yes, it is
Side of the eye	No, it's not
Under the eye	I change my underwear
Under the nose	And that isn't painful
Chin	I change my earrings

Collarbone	And that isn't painful
Under the arm	Well, that's different
Top of the head	No, it's not
Eyebrow	Yes, it is
Side of the eye	Okay, not *all* change is painful
Under the eye	But life change is always painful
Under the nose	Not true
Chin	Yes, it is
Collarbone	No, it's not
Under the arm	Learning to sing wasn't particularly painful
Top of the head	Learning to read wasn't painful
Eyebrow	It was slow
Side of the eye	It took work
Under the eye	But it wasn't painful
Under the nose	Some change can be scary
Chin	But it isn't always painful
Collarbone	In fact, most of the time, it isn't painful
Under the arm	Unless I make it that way
Top of the head	But believing that change is painful
Eyebrow	Is just my subconscious trying to keep me safe and pain free
Side of the eye	And I thank it for its efforts
Under the eye	But maybe I don't need that anymore
Under the nose	I choose to release the expectation that all change is painful
Chin	It is not really true
Collarbone	And that thinking no longer benefits me
Under the arm	Releasing this limiting belief
Top of the head	Releasing this automatic negative and limiting belief

Take note of anything that came up for you in this tapping. Resistance to change is usually multifaceted and likely to involve many past experiences with change that will need additional work. I'd also like to highlight the notion that we can tap to experience more ease or less distress in the change process. This was reflected in many of the positive tapping statements.

Evil

Snakes are seldom portrayed as beacons of happiness and joy. Think about the snakes you have seen in movies or the media. The first movies that pop into my mind are *Anaconda*, the Harry Potter series, and the Indiana Jones movies. The snakes in these movies are representations of evil, danger, or death. It only takes a few minutes of watching the news or looking at social media to know that there is evil in the world we live in, and it can be very distressing. While tapping cannot eliminate evil, it can help us to deal with it better. The next tapping is somewhat general, but you are free to substitute whatever current event is bothering you to make it more effective.

MPI: "Worried about the evil in the world."

Setup (karate-chop point)—Even though I'm worried about this evil in the world, I deeply and completely love and accept myself. Even though I'm worried about this evil in the world, I acknowledge that I cannot change it by worrying more or worrying longer, so I choose to breathe and relax and focus on love, peace, and light. Even though I'm very concerned about the apparent increase of bad things happening in the world, I choose to remain calm and centered.

Eyebrow	All of this evil in the world
Side of the eye	The bad things that are happening
Under the eye	So much chaos
Under the nose	So much hatred
Chin	So many lies
Collarbone	So much disease
Under the arm	So many people are hurting
Top of the head	And being hurt
Eyebrow	All of this evil in the world
Side of the eye	Upset
Under the eye	Scared
Under the nose	Angry
Chin	Worried
Collarbone	About all of the evil in the world
Under the arm	I can't hide from it
Top of the head	But I don't have to let it harm me either

Eyebrow	I can do what I can
Side of the eye	To promote peace, justice, and love
Under the eye	But I have no control over the other people
Under the nose	And worrying will not help
Chin	It can only hurt me
Collarbone	I'm not pretending it doesn't exist
Under the arm	I'm just not wasting energy
Top of the head	All this evil in the world
Eyebrow	But I choose to remain centered
Side of the eye	All of this evil in the world
Under the eye	But I refuse to give it a place inside me
Under the nose	All of this evil in the world
Chin	But I choose not to give it my time
Collarbone	All of this evil in the world
Under the arm	I choose to remain peaceful
Top of the head	I choose to promote love, peace, and light

Wrapping Up

Although I believe that tapping about characteristics of animals for which I have no affinity can be useful, I need to admit that I'm glad to move on to an animal that is less challenging for me. We have tapped on the characteristic of transformation, facing hardships, staying grounded instead of daydreaming, fertility or creation, and the belief that change will be painful. Most of these are areas where I am aware that I need more work, so perhaps that is why I am eager to escape and move on.

I'd like to offer up some snake facts that might be interesting or at least provoke some additional tapping. Snakes eat their prey whole. I find that totally icky, but it could prompt tapping about food and diet issues. A decapitated snake head can still bite for a few hours. This suggests to me some tapping about being alert for continuing danger when the initial crisis is over, or perhaps it might prompt tapping about letting the hyperarousal fade away instead of holding on to it as long as many people do. There are 725 different species of venomous snakes, but only 250 can kill with one bite. This could lead to tapping about the multitude of dangers that are out there or the need to carefully discern which of the possible dangers out there really need our focus.

Some snakes have been known to explode after eating a large meal. I know I have certainly felt like I was going to explode. This snake characteristic might prompt tapping about gluttony, anorexia, or bulimia.

We are going to finish our totem tapping with the wolf. While many characteristics will be similar to those of the dog, there are differences too, and our exposure to these beautiful animals is generally much less. The wolf has been a totem for my dear friend Zach, and when we have been doing energy work together, the wolf has also entered my awareness from time to time.

21
Chapter

Wolf

When I think about the wolf, I get mostly positive feelings. I don't think I would like to run into one in the dark, but I consider them beautiful and majestic creatures. As they are close relatives to dogs, I can't help but think how much I wish I could bury my face in their beautiful fur, scratch those ears, and look deeply into their intelligent eyes. Soon after thinking all of those positive things, the image of the Big Bad Wolf from Aesop's Fables and Grimm's Fairy Tales enters my mind. Shame on that wolf for torturing those poor little pigs.

Sirius, although called the Dog Star, is associated with both dogs and wolves. For example, the ancient Chinese called Sirius the "heavenly wolf." Sirius is part of the constellation *Canis Major*, or the large dog. Sirius was thought to be the home of the gods for the ancient Egyptians and the Dogan tribe in Africa. For the Turkic people, the wolf was believed to be the ancestor of their people.

In Japan, grain farmers once worshipped wolves and left offerings for them because they believed that the wolves could protect their crops from wild boars and deer. Wolf talismans were also used to offer protection from fire and disease and could enhance fertility.

I personally am drawn to the social structure of wolves. I like that they have a strong family structure and that there are rules each member of the pack is expected to follow. Please join me in the tapping meditation about the beautiful wolf.

Tapping Meditation

Eyebrow	Wolf
Side of the eye	Reliance upon instinct
Under the eye	Wolf
Under the nose	Intelligence
Chin	Wolf
Collarbone	Appetite for freedom
Under the arm	Wolf
Top of the head	Social connections
Eyebrow	Wolf
Side of the eye	Passionate living
Under the eye	Wolf
Under the nose	Self-expression
Chin	Wolf
Collarbone	Leadership
Under the arm	Wolf
Top of the head	Family guidance
Eyebrow	Wolf
Side of the eye	Protection
Under the eye	Wolf
Under the nose	Clever
Chin	Wolf
Collarbone	Deep faith
Under the arm	Wolf
Top of the head	Evasive
Eyebrow	Wolf
Side of the eye	Loyalty
Under the eye	Wolf

Under the nose	Proper conduct
Chin	Wolf
Collarbone	What message do you have for me?
Under the arm	Wolf
Top of the head	Open to the message of the wolf

Keep tapping while considering the knowledge, experiences, and meaning that the wolf has for you. Be sure to write down any thoughts, beliefs, or feelings.

I Like Being Part of the Group

Although capable of independence, wolves are generally pack animals. They use the power of the pack for hunting, companionship, and play. A preference for being part of a group isn't generally problematic; however, feeling that you must have a group may not be practical or desirable. Finding balance between being part of a group and independence seems optimal.

MPI: "I need the safety of a pack."

Setup (karate-chop point)—Even though I only move in a pack, just like a wolf, I deeply and completely love and accept my need for the protection and safety of the pack. Even though I feel safer in a pack than I do by myself, I acknowledge and honor this part of who I am. Even though I think the wolf has really got it right by moving in a pack, I am open to the remote possibility that I could be safe by myself, at least some of the time.

Eyebrow	I really identify with the wolf
Side of the eye	They move in packs, just like I do
Under the eye	Packs can be safe
Under the nose	Safety is very important to me
Chin	If my pack isn't around
Collarbone	I can't do anything
Under the arm	But if the pack is around
Top of the head	Things are howlingly perfect
Eyebrow	I've been afraid to stand out from the rest
Side of the eye	I've needed the protection of the group

Under the eye	But just maybe, this isn't true for me anymore
Under the nose	At least not all of the time
Chin	I am open to the remote possibility
Collarbone	That I could be safe by myself, at least some of the time
Under the arm	I might earn more respect from my pack
Top of the head	By demonstrating a little more independence

Identity

Wolves are known for their ability to form strong pack bonds while retaining individuality. They don't lose a sense of who they are while working together for the greater good. Ideally humans would demonstrate this too. Very often, I hear women saying that in the process of marriage and motherhood, they have totally lost a sense of who they are as individual people. The wolf reminds us that both are important to be healthy. We need some balance between individualism and group well-being.

MPI: "I've lost myself."

Setup (karate-chop point)—Even though I feel like I've lost myself, I choose to relax and feel calm. Even though I feel like I've lost my identity, I choose to accept myself and all of these feelings. Even though I feel like I don't know who I am anymore, I choose to honor myself in this struggle.

Eyebrow	I've lost myself
Side of the eye	I don't know who I am any more
Under the eye	It scares me
Under the nose	It makes me sad
Chin	And if I'm really honest, it makes me angry
Collarbone	Not at anyone in particular
Under the arm	Except maybe myself
Top of the head	Taking care of others is important to me
Eyebrow	And people say I'm a good mom because I'm selfless
Side of the eye	But it isn't even a choice anymore
Under the eye	Because it feels like there is no me

Under the nose	Just them
Chin	I know it is not healthy
Collarbone	But to do things for myself
Under the arm	Would decrease what I can do for them
Top of the head	And that doesn't feel okay either

This is another topic that is likely to need more tapping and may have gotten worse with the initial rounds of tapping. If so, try the Gamut Procedure, and then keep tapping with your own words.

Deep Faith

The wolf represents deep faith, not in the sense of contemporary religion, but in terms of divine wisdom or faith in a Great Spirit, who is our teacher and guide. Connection to that Great Spirit can come in many ways. People who are strong in wolf medicine usually are the teachers for the clan. They possess great skill in connecting new ideas with ancient wisdom. The wolf may be telling us to follow a calling for teaching others or urging us to look beyond what we think we know to include seeking new teachers or new experiences for growth. There may be challenges or some anxiety associated with doing that. There may be limiting beliefs. Consider using tapping to move forward or to change your approach as demonstrated in the next tapping sequence, which is constructed around a limiting belief of not being important enough or smart enough to learn from a master teacher or the Great Spirit.

I recently faced a mild version of this feeling when I felt I didn't deserve to take up one of the limited spots in a Zumba class. I would be new to Zumba and might not be able to physically keep up and so didn't feel like I deserved to be there. I am here to attest that tapping helps with that type of negative thinking.

MPI: "I'm not important enough or smart enough to have a master teacher."

Setup (karate-chop point)—Even though I'm not smart enough to learn from a master teacher, I am open to feeling differently about this in the future. Even though I'm not important enough to learn from a master or the Great Spirit, I deeply and completely love and accept myself and am open to feeling differently about this in the future. Even though I'm not smart enough or important enough to learn from a master teacher or the Great Spirit, I choose to love, honor, and respect myself just as I am.

Eyebrow	I'm not smart enough
Side of the eye	Or important enough
Under the eye	For a teacher to bother with me
Under the nose	Why would they?
Chin	It is like they know all of the stuff
Collarbone	And I know nothing
Under the arm	They probably only want to teach
Top of the head	Someone who already knows a lot about this
Eyebrow	If I could even find a teacher
Side of the eye	I wouldn't know what to ask
Under the eye	I'd be too embarrassed
Under the nose	And I couldn't face it if they laughed at me
Chin	Or said no to me
Collarbone	I'm definitely not a candidate for this
Under the arm	And apparently
Top of the head	I think all great teachers are arrogant
Eyebrow	I think all great teachers are rude
Side of the eye	And superior
Under the eye	And apparently mean
Under the nose	No wonder I haven't found a teacher
Chin	If that is what I believe
Collarbone	I believe I am not worthy
Under the arm	And I believe they are all awful
Top of the head	I've set this up for certain failure
Eyebrow	But does it have to be that way?
Side of the eye	Wolf medicine has more faith than that
Under the eye	And hints at a sacred calling
Under the nose	To teach
Chin	And a sacred calling
Collarbone	To learn

Under the arm	Open to changing my viewpoint
Top of the head	Open to learning from anyone who will teach

Having My Own Back

As mentioned before, the wolf is a pack animal. The wolf is also quite capable of managing most situations independently and will definitely defend itself. You could say that while the wolf would benefit from the assistance of others, it will always have its own back. When I was teaching martial arts, we had students who were timid and felt like helpless victims. Most had experienced some sort of bullying or trauma. Once they had the skills to defend themselves, there was a transformation that occurred in their attitudes. They knew they could have their own back.

MPI: "I feel unsafe."

Setup (karate-chop point)—Even though I often feel like I need to protect myself, I choose to honor and respect that part of me. Even though I'm often on high alert and trying to protect myself from real or anticipated threats, I love and respect myself. Even though it sometimes feels pretty crazy to be constantly trying to have my own back all of the time, I love, honor, and accept myself.

Eyebrow	Feeling unsafe
Side of the eye	Always on guard
Under the eye	Evaluating the risk
Under the nose	Looking for danger
Chin	Anticipating what might happen
Collarbone	Seeking assurance of safety
Under the arm	Physical safety
Top of the head	Financial safety
Eyebrow	Emotional safety
Side of the eye	It is all important to me
Under the eye	It has all been threatened before
Under the nose	I never want that again
Chin	So, I analyze

Collarbone	And scan
Under the arm	And try to control whatever I can
Top of the head	In order to be safe

Wrapping Up

In this chapter, we have considered some of the characteristics associated with the wolf. These include being part of a group, finding your identity, deep faith, and the benefit of having your own back. Look back at the tapping meditation to see some other wolf characteristics for your own tapping. Notice both attributes that you would like to enhance and those you might want to tone down. This may change based on what is going on in your life at any given time.

In captivity, wolves have a similar life span to dogs, thirteen to sixteen years. All of the wolves in the pack help to raise and take care of the pups. It apparently isn't considered just women's work. This might spark some tapping about parenting, division of labor, or gender roles. They can roam up to twelve miles a day and can eat twenty pounds of meat each meal. My first thought was that I should tap about walking more so I can eat more. More useful might be some tapping about eliminating avoidance of exercise, increasing movement, or even visiting distant places. As I mentioned before, wolf packs have rules. Perhaps tapping about making rules, breaking rules, or following rules would be beneficial.

22
Chapter

Your Primal Power

Congratulations. You have made it this far. So, what is it you have done? You have completed a variety of tapping exercises, and if you have been tapping along with most, if not all, of them, I would consider you highly skilled in the basics of tapping. I'm sure you no longer have to look at the tapping charts in order to tap (except maybe the Gamut Procedure), and you have probably determined which of the tapping spots seem to be most effective for you. We call that the sweet spot, and you could use it in a pinch, if you needed a quick fix in a difficult moment.

You have also explored characteristics of very real animals. Some of these animals you may have had prior experiences with, and others you may have never even thought much about before. We have explored animals on land, in the sea, and in the air in order to experience a variety of situations, habitats, and vulnerabilities. Obviously, we couldn't cover every animal or every animal behavior, but I trust there were enough different examples for you to find at least one creature that you resonate with and at least one you don't. If you followed instructions, you even have a tapping journal full of animal characteristics that you would like to develop more or less of in your life. I learned so much in the process of researching these animals, and I am hopeful that you are now more interested in exploring the amazing animal kingdom. That is part of the reason for this book, to increase awareness and connection with the natural world.

For each animal, we have also explored some common totem properties as well as relevant mythology from a variety of cultures. Whether you have embraced the idea of animal totems as communication directly to us from nature or Spirit or think of them as more symbolic, it is my sincere hope that you have found consideration of their potential message or meaning a source of inspiration for your own growth.

Most of all, it was my intention that you would learn something about yourself during this process. Not all personal growth or self-development needs to be deadly serious, and it doesn't have to be all that painful or difficult in order to be effective. While extremely beneficial and informative, the use of animals as our starting point has allowed us to take a step back, introduce some playfulness, and open our creativity so that we don't have to approach our own beliefs, thoughts, or behaviors head-on. I know that the head-on approach can be pretty intimidating at times.

I have saved some information to the end because I wanted you to experience the tapping before explaining a little more about the title concepts. If you look up the word *primal* in the dictionary, you generally get two different uses. The first definition is about stages of evolutionary development with *original* as a common synonym. The second definition is "essential" or "fundamental" with *basic, vital, intrinsic,* or *inherent* as synonyms. I developed this book concept with the second definition in mind, but really both are accurate. I see primal power as the source or essence of our personality. It is that essential spark that is inherent in all of us and fundamental to the way we interact in our world. It is that part of us that is untainted by life's hard knocks and is simmering at our core, waiting for expression.

Power is defined as the ability to do something or to take action. Common synonyms include *ability, capacity, potential, capability, and competence.* When you pair the definition of *primal* with the definition of *power* you get an ability or potential for doing great things because of a fundamental essence or inherent characteristic.

Then there is the word *unleash.* That means to release from a leash or similar type of restraint. Common synonyms are *release, free, untie, untether,* or *unshackle.* Combining this with the definitions of *primal* and *power,* this book has been all about helping you to break free of the external and internal forces that have kept you imprisoned or that have made it hard for you to grow into the person you want to become so you can exercise that essential or fundamental ability to act in ways that you choose and desire.

There are a couple of other take-aways specifically about tapping that I want to be sure to highlight.

1. You can't do it wrong. If you miss a tapping point, nothing bad is going to happen. If you spend two minutes at one tapping point and only a few seconds at another, that isn't a problem either. If you do them in a different order, no problem! The tapping points are presented in a specific order just to make it simpler to learn them. You are perfectly free to play around with it, and I predict that as long as you are tapping, you will see results.

2. The words aren't absolutely essential to the process. The words help you to focus on the problem. Many people tap without using any words and get great results. Other people tap with the words and also get great results. Don't let the words stop you from tapping.

3. Warning: things in the mirror may seem larger than they actually are. Sometimes things get a little worse before they get better. We have an amazing ability to shut down uncomfortable emotions, and we have blind spots that we prefer not to correct. When we start tapping, those stuffed emotions might be a little more uncomfortable when you first open them up. Similarly, once those blinders come off, things seem to look a little bigger for a while. You have two choices when that happens. You can either stop tapping for a while and come back to it later, or you can get some professional help if the particular issue seems a little too big to tackle on your own. A little bit of discomfort is okay, but severe emotional pain is probably a sign that you need some assistance.

4. Tap every day. It only takes a minute or two to do a round of tapping. The more frequently you tap (about anything at all), the more likely you are to use this amazing tool when you really need it.

Since beginning to write this book, I have found that I am much more aware of the potential messages from my environment. While I still sometimes plow through my day totally unaware of the animals around me, more often than not, when something seems out of place, unusual, or appears frequently in a short period of time, I stop to consider the possibilities. A useful question is "If this were a message, what could it be?" You don't have to actually believe it is a message; you just have to be willing to speculate. If the possible message fits with something you are dealing with, you have a place to get started with some tapping. If it doesn't seem to fit, don't forget to consider what the opposite message could be. If both don't fit, you've had a cool and interesting experience in thinking about the animal.

Now it is time to get busy and unleash your own primal power.

Happy tapping!

Acknowledgments

I could never have imagined, or completed, a project like this without the inspiration and help of many other people. My parents, my teachers, and my family veterinarian, Ann Bowers, all helped me to develop a love of animals at an early age, and I appreciate my early exposure to birds, dogs, turtles, and fish. I was lucky to have friends who had horses and live near a farm with cows, sheep, and goats. I also happened to be raised in an area where I had pretty easy access to the Cincinnati Zoo and remember visiting there many times.

Thank you to my friend and Reiki master, Zach Keyer, for introducing me to the idea of spirit animals and totems. Zach, you are one of the first people to talk openly to me about a spiritual world outside of formal religion, and I will forever be thankful for your wisdom and friendship. Through Zach, I was introduced to Ted Andrews's books and was fortunate enough to hear him speak on a few occasions and to have a personal animal tarot reading with Ted. I have lost track of the recording from that reading, but my connection to animal spirits was definitely strengthened as a result of that experience.

So many people have inspired my tapping journey. Gary Craig, I am thankful for your generosity in the early years when you made it clear that you wanted tapping in the hands of as many people as possible. When you said to try it on everything, I believed you, and it made a huge difference in my life. Other tapping heroes have also left their mark, including Carol Look, Nick Ortner, Brad Yates, and Rick Wilkes. Carol, I have loved your no-nonsense approach. Nick, I am thankful for the way you have continued to make tapping available to so many people, including the work of your foundation that provides tapping relief to trauma survivors. Brad, your volume of work that you have made available on your own website and on YouTube is amazing and has given me things to tap about when my own creativity wasn't working. Rick, although we have never spoken in person, you have had the most profound impact on the way

I approach tapping for myself and with my clients. Your use of lightheartedness and humor has made tapping much less overwhelming, and because I use it more often, it is more effective.

My family and friends have been supportive throughout the writing process. Joshua, your constant encouragement to pursue my dreams means so much to me. You are not only my son; I am proud to also call you my friend. I love you so much and am incredibly proud of the man you have become. This book would not exist without the help of my friend and partner, Scott Purvis. He has done everything from proofreading, photo editing, and providing technical support for the computer and printers to not complaining when I am grumpy because something isn't going well or holed up in my office for extended periods of time when my creativity is flowing. I cannot express my appreciation enough for all that you do for me.

I have also had a group of friends who were generous with their time to offer constructive feedback for this project, some reading two chapters and others volunteering to read more. Zach, Cyndie, Carol, Tammie, and Grace, each of you helped to make this manuscript better. You also helped me to grow as an author and to get my ego out of the way before going to press.

Cameron Quarles is responsible for the tapping charts in Chapter 1, and also the butterfly and ant drawings. Cameron, thank you for providing illustrations for me. You always seem to know what I want and your contribution to this book was appreciated. Finding the documents that I had not filed properly made you seem like a knight in shining armor.

I'm sure there are people I have forgotten to thank, and I apologize. Know that even if your name didn't make it into the book, you are in my heart.

References

Andrews, Ted. 1999. *Animal-Wise: The Spirit Language and Signs of Nature.* Jackson, TN: Dragonhawk Publishing.

Andrews, Ted. 1999. *The Animal-Wise Tarot.* Jackson, TN: Dragonhawk Publishing.

Andrews, Ted. 2002. *Dreamsong of the Eagle.* Charlottesville, VA: Hampton Roads Publishing Company.

Andrews, Ted. 2002. *Animal-Speak: The Spiritual and Magical Powers of Creatures Great and Small.* St. Paul, MN: Llewellyn Publications.

Bennet, Hal Zina. 2000. *Spirit Animals and the Wheel of Life: Earth-Centered Practices for Daily Living.* Charlottesville, VA: Hampton Roads Publishing Company.

Benyus, Janice M. 1992. Beastly *Behaviors.* Reading, MA: Addison-Wesley Publishing.

Carrington, Patricia. 2001. *How to Create Positive Choices in Energy Psychology: Choices Training Manual.* Kengall Park, NJ: Pace Educational Systems.

Carrington, Patricia. 2008. *Try It on Everything: Discover the Power of EFT.* Bethel, CT: Try It Productions.

Crawford, Gregory. 2002. *Animals in the Stars: Chinese Astrology for Children.* Rochester, VT: Bear Cub Books.

Frankl, Viktor. 2006. *Man's Search for Meaning.* Boston, MA: Beacon Press.

Gallo, Fred P. 2002. *Energy Psychology in Psychotherapy: A Comprehensive Source Book*. New York: W. W. Norton and Company.

Gallo, Fred P., and Harry Vincenzi. 2000. *Energy Tapping: How to Rapidly Eliminate Anxiety, Depression, Cravings, and More Using Energy Psychology*. Oakland, CA: New Harbinger Press.

Meadows, Kenneth. 2002. *Earth Medicine: Explore Your Individuality through the Native American Medicine Wheel*. Edison, NJ: Castle Books.

Morris, Heather. 2018. *The Tattooist of Auschwitz*. New York: Harper Paperbacks.

Noe, Winfried. 1998. *Native American Astrology: The Wisdom of the Four Winds*. New York: Sterling Publishing Co.

Ortner, Jessica. 2014. *The Tapping Solution for Weight Loss and Body Confidence: A Woman's Guide to Stressing Less, Weighing Less, and Loving More*. New York: Hay House Inc.

Ortner, Nick. 2013. *The Tapping Solution: A Revolutionary System for Stress-Free Living*. New York: Hay House Inc.

Ortner, Nick. 2015. *The Tapping Solution for Pain Relief: A Step-by-Step Guide to Reducing and Eliminating Chronic Pain*. New York: Hay House Inc.

Ortner, Nick. 2017. *The Tapping Solution for Manifesting Your Greatest Self: 21 Days to Releasing Self-Doubt, Cultivating Inner Peace, and Creating a Life You Love*. New York: Hay House Inc.

Sams, Jamie, and David Carson. 1999. *Medicine Cards*. Revised, Expanded Edition. New York: St. Martin's Press.

Sanchez, Lynda A. 2014. *Apache Legends and Lore of Southern New Mexico*. Charleston, SC: The History Press.

Thornhill, Jan. 1993. *Crow and Fox and Other Animal Legends*. New York: Simon and Schuster.

Wolpe, Joseph. 1969. *The Practice of Behavior Therapy*. New York: Pergamon Press.

www.Dawsonchurch.com

www.EFTuniverse.com, Church, Dawson

www.emofree.com, Craig, Gary

www.emofree.com, Llewellyn, Mair

www.energypsyched.com, Feinstein, David

www.factretriever.com

www.famu.edu

www.mimimatthews.com (2016) *The Peacock in Myth, Legend, and Nineteenth Century History*

www.native-languages.org

www.primaryhomeworkhelp.co.uk, Barrow, Mandy. "Ancient Egyptian Animals."

www.sunsigns.org

www.thekeep.org, "Animals and the Gods: Sacred Creatures of Egypt"

www.thetappingsolution.com, Prentice, Carol

www.think-differently-about-sheep

www.vega.lpl.arizona.edu, "The Dog Star"

www.whats-your-sign.com/celtic-animals.html, "Celtic Animals and Their Cultural, Symbolic Meanings"

www.wolfmatters.org

Index

About the Author

Dr. Manuel has been responding to the needs of others since her teen years. She began by participating in a youth disaster team and responding to the devastating tornadoes in Xenia, Ohio. That was followed by nursing school at Kettering College of Medical Arts and practicing as an RN in a variety of hospital settings, including the emergency department and oncology research. Later, after receiving a doctoral degree in Clinical Psychology from Wright State University, she managed a private psychology practice and holistic health center for children and adults for many years before migrating to New Mexico.

Although traditionally trained, Dr. Manuel has always blended innovative strategies, such as Reiki, tapping, and therapeutic martial arts with individual and group therapy to improve outcomes and help people move to higher levels of functioning and satisfaction. Although now working in a more traditional health-care setting, she continues to teach others these effective life techniques through her books and other media.

Dr. Manuel is the mother of two handsome, talented, and loving sons, who now have beautiful and loving wives, and is the proud grandmother of a precocious three-year-old granddaughter. She is also the mother to a beautiful daughter, who has lived with her heavenly family since infancy.

Dr. Manuel has a mission to recognize and develop the unique brilliance in every individual with whom she has contact, and that includes you. It is her hope that you will find some morsel, no matter how large or small, that will move you toward a deeper and more satisfying connection with yourself and the Universe. We have the tools at our disposal and now all we have to do is use them. She tells everybody, "Just keep tapping!"

Printed in the United States
By Bookmasters